Simplify Your
Writing Instruction

Simplify Your Writing Instruction

A FRAMEWORK FOR A STUDENT-CENTERED WRITING BLOCK

April Smith

JB JOSSEY-BASS™
A Wiley Brand

For general information on our other products and services or for technical support, please contact our Customer Care Department within the United States at (800) 762-2974, outside the United States at (317) 572-3993 or fax (317) 572-4002.

If you believe you've found a mistake in this book, please bring it to our attention by emailing our reader support team at wileysupport@ wiley.com with the subject line "Possible Book Errata Submission."

Wiley also publishes its books in a variety of electronic formats. Some content that appears in print may not be available in electronic formats. For more information about Wiley products, visit our web site at www.wiley.com.

Library of Congress Cataloging-in-Publication Data is Available:

ISBN 9781394171576 (Paperback)
ISBN 9781394171583 (ePDF)
ISBN 9781394171590 (ePUB)

Illustrator: Christy Smith

Font design: KG fonts

COVER DESIGN: PAUL MCCARTHY
COVER ART: © SHUTTERSTOCK | ARTYWAY

SKY10055578_091923

To my budding writers, Kira & Oliver

CONTENTS

INTRODUCTION

The overwhelming amount of information we filter through each day as teachers is truly incredible. We receive new information from each of our students throughout the day, email back and forth with colleagues and parents, and participate in weekly meetings and training. The internet offers additional information and opportunities for collaboration with teachers around the world. Even when we're not actively working, we're taking in a large number of ideas through online groups and teachers we see in our social media feeds.

With all these resources and ideas at our fingertips, we have a constant stream of ideas for our classrooms. If you're anything like me, you've felt exhausted by the process of trying to piece together ideas into one system that works for your students. It took me years of research and testing ideas in my own classroom before I was able to truly streamline my writing instruction in a way that tailored it to what my students really needed from me. I realized that the best focus of my time during writing instruction was an equal amount of data collection, direct instruction, and support.

When I finally got my writing instruction system down, people started to notice. Other teachers in my building asked me what I was doing, and a few inquired about how I was able to fit in any writing time at all. Up until that point, I thought I was the only one who struggled with teaching writing. After sharing with teachers in my building, and ultimately working with new teachers through district writing training, I realized there are many teachers who are in constant search of a simple system for writing instruction that works for their classroom.

Without a focused system in place for writing time, both teachers and students can become overwhelmed with the process. Writing is not a solvable problem you can answer in a few minutes. It takes time to discuss, research, and plan even a short writing piece. This can often make writing a frustrating and tedious activity for everyone if it's not broken into manageable pieces. This barrier creates an environment that doesn't foster growth. It doesn't leave much room for the teacher to help students fill in their individual gaps in learning, nor does it allow time for the student to apply new skills.

When feelings of being overwhelmed arise, we tend to either overcompensate by adding more to our writing block, or we push it aside for later. However, we can't push aside something this important. Teaching students to write equips them with fundamental skills that are *essential* for success in almost all aspects of life. It is not only about getting words on paper by the end of their writing time. The skills we model during the writing block also help them develop critical thinking, communication, and creativity skills that support all other subject areas in your classroom. We also can't add more to our block because it adds to our feelings of being overwhelmed.

There is a desperate need for us to bring the focus back on basic writing skills, but putting the research behind writing instruction into a system that works in a real classroom is a challenge. This is why I decided to write this book with a heavy focus on simple and efficient differentiation. We need ways to reach all our students that don't require us to create 30 different lessons. This book includes simple processes for you to put into place in your classroom, building a student-centered writing block one step at a time.

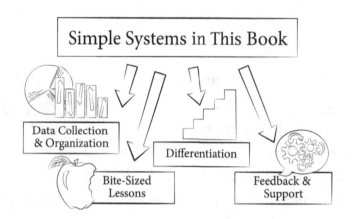

Before we move into the process, it's important to note that the tools and strategies in this book have been tested with students in second grade and above. Some methods in this book do work well in K–1 classrooms, but the system was not created for these grade levels.

Another important thing to keep in mind as you work through this book is that this is a year-long process. You should not try to put every system in place all at once. We teach students small skills that build upon each other, and we give them time to practice before progressing to the next skill. You should approach this process the same way. Some teachers may find themselves trying small group in the second month, while others aren't comfortable until they've had an entire quarter to practice the mini-lesson and writing block procedures. Implement this system at your own pace.

Many organizers are included with this book, but it's unlikely that you'll use them all. In each section, I encourage you to use only the ones that are appropriate for the writing type you're working on and meet the needs of your students. Apart from the pre-assessment, which is a non-negotiable, don't use something if you or your students don't need it. This process is all about helping students fill in learning gaps and find success with writing in a simple way.

The link icon (⊚) means there is a downloadable resource available that goes with the chapter. You can create a free account and access these resources by visiting:
`https://www.simplifywriting.com/book-resources`.

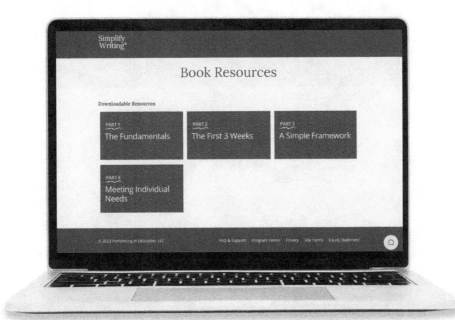

Simplify Your
Writing Instruction

PART ONE

THE FUNDAMENTALS

CHAPTER 1

Common Struggles

When I was a new teacher struggling with writing instruction, I felt like it was my fault because I struggled with writing in school myself. I was embarrassed to admit that I didn't really know how to teach writing. I went to a great teacher preparation program and was passionate about teaching, so why were my students struggling to even write a paragraph?

It took me years to realize that I was not alone in my struggle to teach writing. Now, I receive multiple emails daily from teachers who found my website while searching for solutions. It's important to understand the reasons we have these struggles so that we can create a plan that addresses or works around them.

TIME

Why do we struggle so much to fit writing time in? In many schools, the focus on math and reading has left limited time for other subjects. We continue to extend the math and reading blocks to keep up with expanding standards and state testing. Because students can write in every subject, it's easy to say, "We can incorporate writing into the other subjects, so there's no need for a dedicated time." Even many textbook companies are producing English Language Arts (ELA) curriculum that incorporates reading and writing, but the writing seems like an afterthought.

When I opened up our ELA textbooks my first year, it seemed very straightforward. My students would read and answer questions, and then they would write about what they read. I couldn't understand why my students were struggling to write. It was years later when I realized that our ELA curriculum only included the *application* of writing, with no lessons for me to actually teach the skills they needed to do this writing.

Several years later, I was exposed to my first actual writing curriculum. It made sense to take the time to teach them how to write. But that was the real issue – time. I had hour-long writing lessons in my hands, but a 90-minute ELA block with reading curriculum that took at least that long. The solution, I was told, was to teach writing when I could fit it in and incorporate more writing application into all the other subject areas. That left me again without consistent time for actual writing lessons.

Although integration is a great time-saver and is important for students to apply their writing skills, it doesn't always leave room for the direct instruction they need. When students are only receiving sporadic writing lessons, they don't become confident writers. When you mix this with complex content vocabulary and technical information, it's a recipe for disaster for our struggling students. Studies strongly support having a dedicated writing time where students can receive adequate practice and instruction in writing. Writing skills are sorely lacking in many schools because there is no explicit writing instruction (Graham, 2019).

The systems in this book have been used in many classrooms where time was limited, including my own. Through a lot of trial and error, I learned that I could teach writing with limited time, but I absolutely needed a dedicated writing block where I taught a short whole group lesson and students applied what they learned in their own writing immediately after. Only then were my students able to apply those new skills to reading, math, science, and social studies.

So, how much time do you need? It really depends on the individual situation, but I have some common schedules that I suggest. If you can do 45 minutes a day of writing, that is fantastic. More realistically, a lot of teachers I work with do 30 minutes a day or 45 minutes three times a week. My middle school teachers with only 50 minutes a day to teach ELA often block out time for two full writing units each quarter, and then they teach reading standards while having students apply their newly acquired writing skills the rest of the time. We'll discuss schedule and the writing block in Part III so that you can create something that works for your unique situation.

VARYING STUDENT ABILITY LEVELS

By far, the most difficult task teachers have is teaching grade-level standards when our students are all at completely different levels. Your classroom is made up of below, at, and above grade-level students. You probably have students with learning disabilities, second language learners, and gifted students.

I have upper-elementary and middle school teachers contact me on a daily basis asking what to do with a handful of students who can't write a sentence or a paragraph, which is a challenge when their on-level writing lessons are focused on multiparagraph pieces. This situation is all too common in our classrooms. This is why I decided to write this book with a focus on simple and efficient differentiation that any teacher can implement.

The word *differentiation* can cause a panic for many teachers. With limited time and resources, it's hard enough to fit in one whole group lesson. Adding different types of lessons and strategies for different learners can seem impossible. Differentiation is not individualized learning in the sense that a different lesson needs to be made for every student. Instead, it offers multiple types of learning when working with students in whole group, small group, and individually during writing conferences. Differentiation, done correctly, means making proactive modifications to your regular units that meet the needs of your students (Tomlinson, 2017).

The strategies built into each part of this book are what will address your students' need for more support. You will still have students at varying ability levels, but you'll have the tools you need to differentiate for all of them. You'll learn how to naturally differentiate your lessons to reach your special education, English Language Learner (ELL), gifted students, and everyone in between.

My biggest challenge teaching students with different writing abilities and goals is preparing and organizing lessons that are at their instructional level. The grade-level curriculum provided did not meet the individual needs of my students. The lower grade levels did not teach the correct content, and the higher grade levels did not include the foundational writing skills my students were missing. I was constantly searching for strategies, mini-lessons, and activities for my students. I also had to have additional activities prepared for my paras who were running small groups and working 1:1 with students.

– Holli Duncan, Special Education Teacher

LACK OF TRAINING AND CURRICULUM

Many new teachers find themselves ill-equipped to effectively teach writing to their students due to a lack of comprehensive instruction during their college years. While teacher education programs may cover the basics of writing instruction, they often fail to provide in-depth training on the intricacies of teaching writing as a complex and multifaceted skill. As a result, many teachers feel unprepared to address the diverse needs of their students, including different writing genres, individual writing processes, and strategies for providing meaningful feedback.

After teachers graduate from their respective programs, they continue to receive general training sessions from their school district. I think that most of us can agree that writing is not an easy subject to teach, yet most schools don't provide in-depth professional development that supports teachers in this endeavor. This isn't to say that school administrators don't want their teachers or students to succeed in writing. They are limited by time and resources just like teachers are. This often leads to quick trainings on one novel strategy that they can add to what they're already doing. For many teachers, there is no complete system for writing instruction provided, leaving them confused and discouraged about why what they're doing isn't working in the classroom.

We also have a lot of inconsistency when it comes to writing curriculum. Some schools have ELA curriculum with a heavy focus on reading and no explicit writing skill instruction. Other schools implement do-it-yourself (DIY) strategies by collecting lessons from workbooks and the internet. There are some schools that have quality writing curriculum with no training on how to use it. For teachers who do not know how to teach writing, having a poor curriculum, or none at all, can be extremely stressful.

 My biggest struggle was coming in as a new ELA teacher with no curriculum. I had to piece-meal several things to create a lesson. Nothing was cohesive, and I had no time for my family – for my own children – because I was always lesson planning or grading. I also had no idea how to teach writing. Writing is something that came naturally to me, but teaching how to write is a completely different ball game.

– Frauline Walker, 6th-Grade Teacher

So, what is a "quality" writing curriculum? Most importantly, it must include structured writing mini-lessons that consider the limited time teachers have to teach writing and the varying ability levels of their writers. While having structured lessons, the flexibility in how and when the lessons are delivered is key to properly differentiate. If you don't have a curriculum like this, don't panic. This book will provide you with the tools to make the modifications you need for success.

If you feel like lack of training or curriculum is a big issue in your school, consider bringing in other teachers and administrators by starting a book study with this book. Chances are, there are many other teachers in your building who struggle with teaching writing.

ADDRESSING THESE STRUGGLES

I've given training on my systems to over 50,000 teachers, which has allowed me the opportunity to see how it works in a lot of different classrooms. I've learned that there is no one system or program that works *exactly* the same way in every classroom. I joke that I "differentiate to help teachers differentiate." This is why you'll see different options and modifications listed in each chapter. These systems need to be tailored to your constraints and what your current group of students need.

In future chapters, we will lay the foundation for streamlining your lessons while incorporating simple differentiation techniques to help reach students of all ability levels. Putting these basic foundations in place (in a way that works for your class) is key in addressing the struggles we have discussed in this chapter. Once you feel like you have these down, you can move on to more complex strategies like small group and conferring.

Before moving forward, I strongly recommend you either use a notebook or a document on your computer, tablet, or cell phone to take notes on key takeaways and your tasks going forward. Throughout the book, journal boxes are included where I ask you to stop and set an intention or goal. You may also want to go back to reread this journal and the corresponding section of the book as you implement each part and prepare for the next step.

CHAPTER 2

What Really Matters

There's an overwhelming amount of information about writing instruction online and in print. It can be incredibly difficult to figure out where to start, what things to do (or not do), and what you can actually fit into your tight schedule. I once observed a teacher who had completely different systems in place each time I came in. It was hectic, to say the least. When things didn't work for her students, she'd change absolutely everything in hopes that the next idea she saw on Pinterest would stick. Not only did it add a lot of prep time she didn't have, but it was confusing and frustrating her students. We don't need fancy or creative activities to teach writing. We need to focus on a few key things that *really* matter.

HAVING SIMPLE SYSTEMS IN PLACE

When it comes to the organization and management of your writing block, simple and efficient systems are important. Nothing in this book requires you to create or prep anything time-consuming. You may think, "April, this is basic common sense," a few times throughout the book. That's because we don't need anything complicated in our writing blocks. We're going to cut out a lot of unnecessary activities from our lessons and focus more on what engages our students and meets their individual needs.

UTILIZING DATA

I'll admit that, at one time, I would cringe any time I heard the word *data* in a meeting. Every year, it seemed like we had more and more testing to gather data on our students. I personally felt a disconnect between gathering data and actually utilizing it. When we gave pre-assessments at the beginning of the year, I would get back a list of overall scores. The most I could gather from this data was which kids may struggle in a subject overall. I couldn't pinpoint the exact learning gaps that they had.

Do not feel discouraged by the word *data* and skip the systems in Part II of the book. If you have negative connotations for the word, replace it with "information gathering" instead. There is a difference between collecting scores and meaningful information gathering. I don't have much use for a single test score assigned to a student in my class, but I do have a use for specific information like Bobby struggles with paragraph structure and my class as a group has poor writing stamina.

The next part of this book is all about gathering and recording data in a **meaningful** way. It is much easier to set up your students for success when you know up front exactly what gaps they have in their writing skills. We often miss the mark with data-led instruction because we don't have the right pre-assessment or a good system to use the data we gather. I'm going to provide you with a simple, engaging pre-assessment, and I'm going to walk you through exactly how to evaluate learning gaps and organize the data to actually put it into use. You'll have one simple spreadsheet with data to use as you plan your lessons and modify instruction to meet the needs of each writer.

UNCOMPLICATED "BITE-SIZED" LESSONS

When we struggle with time, we often try to cram as many skills as possible into each lesson. This leads to a lot of stress and confusion for us and our students. Chapter 9 discusses how to split the writing process into efficient and effective 10- to 15-minute mini-lessons. This chapter also covers what to do next to optimize student output after each lesson, as well as a few strategies you may be doing during your lessons that you can cut out. You'll also learn what elements you *should* include to engage all of your students during your whole group lesson.

FILLING IN GAPS USING DIFFERENTIATION

Differentiation is the "secret sauce" to help fill in the gaps and see growth from your writers. However, it can be a struggle to differentiate without needing more time for planning, preparation, and implementation. Throughout the book, I teach you the easiest ways to modify content for your students, including natural differentiation opportunities you can build into your whole group lessons. It's all about working smarter, not harder, when it comes to meeting varying student needs.

PROVIDING FEEDBACK AND SUPPORT

Our students need consistent feedback to improve upon their writing, but we don't exactly have time to confer one-on-one with each student every week. In Part IV, I offer a few simple systems to try in your classroom to make feedback simple and more authentic. Not only will this amplify your students' writing skills, but it will teach them real-world skills they can use to gain new ideas and improve upon their work for decades to come.

 I find that I am in the minority when I say I LOVE teaching writing. However, that doesn't mean that the instruction is without its challenges. I have tried to focus more on working with small groups, and individuals during conferences in a more differentiated model. I still struggle with what to focus on during these conferences, without having a "fix everything" mindset. I remember hearing to never take the pencil from the student, or it becomes YOUR writing piece. I continually remind myself of this when feeling like I might not be getting my conference point across. Breathe deeply; hands off the student pencil!

– Wendy Farris, 3rd-Grade Teacher

With limited time, most teachers can't even imagine being able to use small group instruction during the writing block. I offer ways to help fill in the individual learning gaps your students have with intentional, well-organized small group lessons. This only works once you have the other systems in place in your writing block, but it's well worth the wait.

Throughout this book, I provide the simple strategies you need to put these five items into place. However, none of this can happen without you deciding to make writing a priority in your classroom. In the next chapter, I discuss the simple steps you should take to create your consistent, dedicated writing block.

CHAPTER 3

Make Writing a Priority

Having a dedicated writing block is essential for teaching students the skills they need to become proficient writers. It allows for explicit learning time by providing the necessary time to focus on specific writing techniques, strategies, and skills. Without this time, there's no opportunity to provide direct instruction, model good writing, and provide opportunities for students to practice and apply what they've learned.

Second, having a dedicated writing block helps establish a routine that leads to better overall writing output. Routines help create smooth transitions between activities and therefore allow fewer opportunities for disruptions to occur (Burden, 2003). Routines are most effective when they are consistent, explicit, and teach students in a direct and systematic way. By setting aside a specific time each day to write, writers can develop a routine that allows them to be more productive and efficient in their writing.

This dedicated time also provides an opportunity for you to give individualized feedback, which is crucial for student growth and development. This time can also be used to provide differentiated instruction to meet the needs of all students and help them to achieve their full potential as writers. None of this can be done when writing is integrated into a block of time where writing instruction is not the focus.

MY STORY

Five years into my teaching career, I was still struggling to fit writing into my ELA block. I was departmentalized for the first time, and the short periods made it impossible for me to steal time from another subject area like I had in prior years. I had time-consuming reading curriculum and a binder of random writing materials to refer to for writing. I had zero training on how to teach writing. I checked off every struggle that is listed in Chapter 1.

I knew I needed to make a change. If I continued to simply cram in a writing unit whenever I had time, my students were going to leave my class without the ability to write more than a paragraph. So, I decided that I was going to teach a full writing unit each month.

This led to me carving out one week every month to focus solely on writing. I was teaching the entire writing process in five days. It helped, but not as significantly as I had expected. My students showed better organization when writing, but they still struggled with revision, editing, and elaboration. We were all rushed. After three weeks passed, and we moved on to the next unit, it was like we were starting over at square one. I realized that my students needed more consistent instruction and practice time.

I decided to take a more drastic step and carve out an actual writing block in my classroom. In my 90-minute ELA block, I decided that I would try to incorporate writing for 30 minutes, five times a week.

WHAT I LEARNED

I learned so much from my new dedicated writing block. At first, I learned that it's difficult to teach a lesson and have student practice time in 30 minutes without having some key procedures in place. I tightened up my writing block using the strategies that are discussed in Chapter 9. Then, I learned that my students were at drastically different ability levels. It took me a couple of months to really figure out what each student needed (see Part II of this book to avoid this lengthy learning process).

After six months of my dedicated writing block, our lessons were running efficiently. I was starting to find joy in teaching writing, and my students seemed to feel the same way. I even started to reuse some of our writing lessons and organizers when writing during our reading block. Before I started teaching students *how* to write, they were struggling to write about their reading. I realized that integration of writing into the other subject areas is crucial, but it can never be standalone. Direct writing instruction is a necessity.

I also started to notice a transformation in not only the way my students wrote, but their attitude about writing. This spread to the other subject areas, benefiting students' ability to express themselves across the board.

I noticed that:

- My students felt more confident and prepared to tackle writing tasks in other subject areas.
- My students enjoyed writing for the first time in years.
- I was able to help my below grade level students see growth and feel successful.

I am a brand new teacher when it comes to writing. Having a dedicated writing block each day has helped me and my students blossom. For instance, we started simply brainstorming at the beginning of the new year in January. Now we are a month into the process, and we are confidently creating our own class book on kindness with illustrations. It is titled "Be Kind."

– Roz P. Chantengco, K–6 Online Independent Study Teacher

WHAT THIS MEANS FOR YOU

All our classrooms are unique, so no one specific strategy or setup will work for everyone. However, simply carving out a dedicated writing block has been the biggest game-changer for the teachers whom I work with. **If you do not have a dedicated time to implement the strategies in this book, the system will not work.**

Your schedule doesn't need to be exactly the same as mine. It just needs to be **consistent** and have **adequate time** for direct instruction and student practice. In Part III, I help you create a schedule that works for your class. For some teachers, it's a matter of splitting up the ELA block to better balance reading and writing time. For others, time needs to be carved out somewhere else. You need to make writing a priority in your classroom if you want to see long-lasting results.

Once you start consistently teaching writing lessons using the strategies in this book, you'll find yourself excited to incorporate writing application into your other subject areas. I encourage you to do this in an authentic way. Incorporate discussion, research, and writing application into the other subject areas in a way that is natural and not repetitive. You'll also find that students are able to communicate better on paper and verbally when they become more confident in their writing skills. It's a win all around!

You may also find it beneficial to encourage students to find natural ways to practice their writing skills at home. A letter home like the one included in the Appendix can help provide parents with ways to get their child writing. Instead of sending home writing homework, you can encourage students to work on writing at home that matches their interests. The list on the take-home letter has a lot of great ideas!

Remember, this process is a journey. Implement each part of this book in order and take the time you need to try it and reflect. Even with limited time, it's essential you do the pre-assessment, observation, and recording in Part II. That information is necessary to use the differentiation techniques that come after your basic writing system is in place. Most of all, give yourself some grace when things don't go the way that you expect. Ten years later, I am still learning and making small changes to make the process work for different groups of students. You will find what works for you through this process, and with consistency, you'll see your own professional growth and the growth in students' writing abilities that you've been working toward.

You may be tempted to add additional elements to your writing block while you're beginning to implement the strategies in this book. If you see another teacher doing something interesting, reflect on if you have the time or resources to incorporate it before adding it to your plate. It's unlikely that you do, and it may detract from putting the systems from this book in place. Once you feel comfortable with the basic systems that matter, you can start to experiment with adding new components to your writing block.

Reflect and Plan

Set an intention for how you will make writing a priority in your classroom. Write to your students' parents about what these changes might look like in your classroom. A Sample Letter Home is located in the Appendix as well as for download.

⊘ File D3.1 Sample Letter Home Reproducible

PART TWO

THE FIRST
THREE WEEKS

The first three weeks of your new writing system are the most crucial. You'll not only be collecting the data that will drive your lesson planning for the rest of the year, but you'll be identifying some major issues that need to be addressed before beginning your regular units. Three weeks may seem like a lot of time before you can get into your regular writing blocks, but I promise you that these weeks will help make your lessons more successful and efficient in the long run. If you've felt like many of your students really struggle to grasp your on-grade level lessons, it's even more imperative you take the time to complete the simple steps in this section.

If you've picked up this book mid-year, follow the same process as if it were the first three weeks of school. It's not unheard of for me to pause and reassess my students if I feel like their growth is stagnant. There's nothing wrong with you doing the same in order to identify the skill gaps that are getting in the way of your students succeeding.

It may be tempting to skip this section and go straight into the framework for your regular lessons, but your writing block will be anything but simple without this part in place. The truth is, if your students struggle with writing in your classroom now, not much will change if you don't have the information and plan in place to help them. You'll continue to spin your wheels, which won't save you any time in the long run.

Week 1	Weeks 2–3	Week 4
Pre-assess, observe, and record	Set the building blocks of your lesson by addressing major issues	Begin your regular writing unit with necessary modifications

CHAPTER 4

The Power of Informal Pre-Assessment

Pre-assessment is important because it allows for you to determine the prior knowledge and skill level of your students. This information is crucial to help adjust your instruction to meet the needs of your students and ensure you are providing appropriate learning experiences. By identifying students' prior knowledge, you also can find gaps in their understanding and provide targeted instruction to help fill those gaps.

It's imperative for you to have pre-assessment data to be able to set learning goals and objectives for your students. By assessing student writing abilities, you can identify areas where students need to improve and set specific, measurable, and achievable goals to guide instruction. This helps you ensure your whole group instruction is focused and aligned with students' needs and students are making progress toward meeting their learning goals. It's the best tool you can have when planning your upcoming writing units.

Additionally, pre-assessment can also set the stage for you to monitor individual student progress and form small groups when you're ready. It can also help you provide individual feedback to students, which is essential if you want to confer with students. It's also extremely helpful in many grading systems, such as mastery-based grading.

Pre-assessment has been my No. 1 tool for overcoming my struggles with writing instruction. We know that students have knowledge gap and varying ability levels. An informal pre-assessment where your students write for enjoyment allows for you to observe what they can do, where they will struggle in the upcoming year, and how they feel about writing. In this chapter, we reimagine what writing pre-assessment should look like in your classroom to get real, meaningful data, not just a score.

WHY PRE-ASSESS AT ALL IF TIME IS AN ISSUE?

One common question I get from teachers is: Why not just skip the pre-assessment and use the valuable time for more instruction? The data from the pre-assessment allows for your future instruction time to be *much* more impactful. If you follow the process that is laid out in this chapter, you will have concrete information on every single student's writing needs, and a simple plan for how to meet the varying student ability levels.

Teachers who pre-assess *with the objective of observing gaps in knowledge and student struggles*:
- Go into their first writing lesson feeling more confident and prepared.
- Are able to better meet the needs of struggling writers.
- Have a better idea of student progress and growth throughout the year.

Assessments should have a purpose if we're going to use instructional time. Not only will you use this data to tailor your units to your whole group, but you'll use it to start planning how to fill in individual learning gaps. You'll also use this data to start tracking student growth.

WHAT PRE-ASSESSMENT SHOULD LOOK LIKE

A common misconception is that you can only gather important data from "big" summative assessments (Venables, 2014). Throughout this book, you'll learn to gather meaningful data in many ways. None of those ways is a formal test because it's not necessary to give one to get the data you need to make a plan of action for your writers.

The best pre-assessment is the simplest and meets the least amount of resistance. The more formal you make the pre-assessment, the easier it is for students to get "stuck." Kids know when something is a test, and they don't always perform their best when it's a test on something they know they struggle with. By removing the stressors of a formal test, we give them the best chance to show us what they can *really* do.

Spend the first five days of your new writing block with informal writing time where students respond to a variety of prompts. If your students can't write for as long as suggested, less time is perfectly fine. The point of this activity is to collect data, and knowing that your class can't write for an extended period is important information.

The Simple Pre-Assessment Process:

1. Gather five high-interest writing prompts. If your students are very resistant to writing, find out their interests and tailor the writing prompts to those. To do this, gather your students together and make a list of their interests before you write your custom prompts. You may choose a variety of writing types to see how students tackle the different styles.

2. Get students excited about writing. Feel free to let them discuss the prompts with their friends before writing (this is always encouraged!), draw pictures, use fun pens. Remember, **this is not a test.**

3. Have students write informally, to respond to one prompt each day, either in a notebook or a document on their device. Keep each student's samples together. You don't want to be opening five files or sorting paper when you go to review the samples.

4. Write down anything important you observe during this pre-assessment time. (See the next chapter for some examples of "big picture" items that you may observe during the journaling time.)

5. Set aside a couple of hours to review each student's writing samples. (See the next chapter for how to observe and record important information from student samples.)

This informal pre-assessment **should not:**
- Use privacy folders or have the feeling of testing.
- Be a stuffy formal writing process where students are expected to follow certain steps or use specific organizers.
- Lack discussion or engagement.
- Make students feel stressed about writing.

Recommended Daily Pre-Assessment Time

2nd–3rd Grade
10–15 minutes

4th–5th Grade
15–20 minutes

Middle School
20–30 minutes

THE PURPOSE BEHIND USING MULTIPLE PROMPTS

I am often asked why I use five prompts instead of letting students focus on creating a full writing piece over the week. Having a new writing prompt each day allows for students to have a fresh start. If you only collect one writing piece, your data may be skewed by disinterest in or lack of background information about the prompt. If the student is having a bad day the first day or is overwhelmed, it's harder for them to catch up the rest of the week. By collecting five different samples, we can get a better overall picture of what our students can do.

Another benefit to using five different prompts is being able to see samples of different types of writing. You may notice that your students really thrive at writing narratives, but they get stuck when writing informational text. You might observe that students enjoy writing narratives, but they don't use any dialogue (or they use it incorrectly). This is all important information to use in our planning as we prepare for our units.

Sample Elementary Prompts

Monday	Tuesday	Wednesday	Thursday	Friday
Some days go better for us than others. Think of a day that you might have called "The BEST Day Ever" or "The WORST Day Ever." Write about it. Be sure to include everything that will help your reader feel the emotions of your best or worst day ever.	Movies and video games are very popular. Choose a movie or video game and explain it to someone who has never heard of it before. Other option: Choose a book.	Think of someone in your life who deserves to get a medal for kindness. Why does that person deserve to get a medal?	Think about an animal you know a lot about. What characteristics does it have that help it to survive in its environment? Think about how it gets around, gets its food, stays safe, etc. Write a few paragraphs to teach someone about how your animal can survive in its environment.	Tell the story of when your main character finally brings home the pet they've been begging for.

Sample Middle School Prompts

Monday	Tuesday	Wednesday	Thursday	Friday
Trying something for the first time can be exciting or intimidating. Think about a time you tried something new. Write a narrative about what happened and how you felt. Use first-person point of view, sensory details, and dialogue to tell your story.	A good teacher can make a positive impact on a student's life. Explain the qualities of an effective teacher.	As children grow up, they learn to take care of themselves and be more self-reliant. At which age should kids be allowed to stay home by themselves? State your claim with evidence to support your reasons.	Being healthy is important for feeling good and living a long life. Think of some of the different ways people try to improve their physical health. Write a few paragraphs informing others of at least three things they can do to maintain a healthy lifestyle.	A family takes a road trip, but its car breaks down along the way. Write a creative narrative about how the family makes it to its destination and what happens along the way.

Don't expect to get back fully completed and polished writing pieces each day. The skills we will be observing when we look at these samples don't require a complete piece. In the next chapter, you learn exactly what we're looking for in our samples, and it's not a grade from a rubric! We're going to take a much deeper dive into the student writing pieces to make an individualized plan that sets you and your students up for success.

One of the cornerstones of creating a student-centered writing block is differentiating instruction. Differentiation is easier when you have pre-assessment data. By understanding the unique needs and abilities of each student, you can tailor instruction to meet the needs of your students as a group and individually. Pre-assessment data is an essential tool for setting student goals and differentiating instruction to meet the needs of all students.

PRE-ASSESSMENT FAQs

WHAT IF I'M STARTING THIS MID-YEAR?

If you're reading this book mid-year, you're probably at your wit's end trying to create a writing block that works for you and your students. This is why you should *not* skip the pre-assessment. It is perfectly fine at any time in the school year to stop and say, "What I am doing is not working, so I need to re-assess my systems and learn where my students are struggling."

SHOULD THE OUTPUT EACH DAY BE A FULL WRITING PIECE?

Think of students' response to these prompts as informal as journaling. Some of your students may write a paragraph in the time you give them, while others may produce a few organized paragraphs. You're not going to get polished pieces, but you will get valuable information on where your students struggle.

SHOULD I GIVE THESE PIECES A GRADE?

My opinion is that these pieces should not be graded since students are using their current skills, and I haven't done anything to provide them with instruction or support beforehand. That being said, I understand grading them if you're required to put a grade in the gradebook for the week.

HOW MUCH TIME SHOULD I ALLOW STUDENTS TO WRITE?

The amount of time students write will really vary from one child to the next. This is why I set aside 15–20 minutes and see what happens. If my class is really into writing and wants longer, I'll use the entire block. More often than not, they struggle to write for even 15 minutes. This is very important information for my future planning.

WHAT IF I HAVE STUDENTS WHO JUST WON'T WRITE?

If you've tried absolutely everything to make the process engaging and low stress, you may still have a student who can't, or won't, write. This can be very frustrating, but look at it as an opportunity to find out why they aren't writing. It is so much better to explore these issues and create a plan for the student before you're teaching your actual lessons.

WHAT IF STUDENTS WRITE A FEW SENTENCES AND STOP?

This is also an opportunity to find out why students have this limitation and determine how you can address it. You can encourage them to keep writing, but make sure to note which students struggle with writing stamina. I talk more about writing stamina in the next chapter.

WHAT ABOUT MY ELL STUDENTS?

It's essential to know what language skills your English Language Learners (ELLs) have so that you can support them during your on-grade-level lessons. Read the prompts aloud to these students and answer any questions they have. If they're unable to write in English, take a note of it and allow them to write in their native language so that they can still participate.

SHOULD I GIVE STUDENTS INSTRUCTION ON EXPECTATIONS FOR THEIR WRITING PIECE BEFOREHAND?

There's no need to give any formal lessons, but you can facilitate discussion and talk about what students can include in their writing if they need a little extra help to get started.

SHOULD THEY TYPE OR HANDWRITE?

Have students complete the pre-assessment in the same manner that they will be writing during your regular lessons. If your students will be using technology, it's so important to evaluate where they may struggle with it.

Reflect and Plan

When and how will you pre-assess your students? Pull out your calendar and set the dates and times when you will give students the time to respond to five engaging prompts.

CHAPTER 5

Make Observations and Record Important Data

We often pre-assess in the beginning of the year to track growth along a few data points throughout the year. Although there isn't anything necessarily wrong with this, most upper-elementary and middle school pre-assessments aren't set up to give us the specific details we need to create a differentiation plan for our students. We're missing a big opportunity to gather actionable data when all we do is record a score.

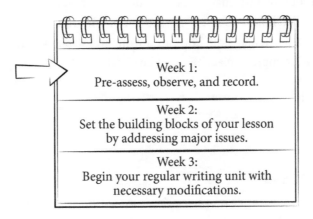

Week 1:
Pre-assess, observe, and record.

Week 2:
Set the building blocks of your lesson by addressing major issues.

Week 3:
Begin your regular writing unit with necessary modifications.

WHAT IS ACTIONABLE DATA?

Actionable data is any information you can use to immediately act on in your classroom. A single score can tell you where students are on scale, but it can't tell you what areas students are struggling in or where they need to be challenged. Even if you use a rubric where you score different areas of the writing piece, it's leaving out a lot of important information. This is why this part of the system is the most impactful on the success of your writing block.

I've had teachers contact me because their students were struggling, and they couldn't pinpoint the exact reasons. My first question is always: "Can you share your pre-assessment spreadsheet?" On many occasions, the teacher did the pre-assessment, but used a rubric to score it for a grade instead of recording the specific writing skills into the recording spreadsheet. As teachers, we often allow people to talk us out of important steps, or we feel forced to take shortcuts to save time. If you need to get a score or use a district rubric, please do, but **do not skip the step where you get the data you need to act on differentiating your writing block.**

So, what are you looking for exactly? You're looking for any "Big Picture" items that will slow down your students when you get to your writing units. You're also looking for gaps in major technical skills that will make the writing process a struggle. This data will allow you to immediately take action by implementing lessons that fill in these major gaps and set the building blocks for your regular writing units.

Specific and Actionable Writing Pre-Assessment Data	
"Big Picture" Items	**Technical Skills**
Writing Stamina	Sentence & Paragraph Writing
Attitude toward Writing	Writing Structure
Interests	Complexity of Ideas (Idea Generation & Elaboration)
	Conventions (Grammar & Spelling)
	Technology Knowledge

As we continue through this chapter, I'll show you exactly what to record for each of these items. You'll also be recording individual student struggles for later in the process when you're ready to implement simple small group lessons to begin filling in individual learning gaps. The spreadsheet in this chapter will be your best friend for the pre-assessment recording process and continuing to monitor the skills your students need extra help on.

The best part of this spreadsheet is that, throughout the year, you'll be able to look at it while you're planning each upcoming unit. The information on the spreadsheet will help prepare you for the skills your students will struggle with. You'll find yourself making simple modifications like extending a basic lesson to add in extra supports for a particular skill. You can download the blank spreadsheet using the link at the beginning of this book. The Example Spreadsheet can be viewed in the Appendix.

⊚ File D5.1 Blank Spreadsheet
⊚ File D5.2 Example Spreadsheet

THE RECORDING PROCESS

Now that you've had a peek at our simple pre-assessment spreadsheet, let's break down when and how you'll enter your data. Even before you officially begin the pre-assessment prompts, you'll be taking a pulse on your class's attitude toward writing. Record anything you notice about students' reaction to preparing to write. Do they know what supplies they need? Are they stressed about the prospect of writing? Are they excited and ready to write?

Their attitude about writing may not be a skill-based observation, but it's something you absolutely need to be aware of. There are some simple ways to tweak your lessons to get buy-in from your reluctant writers. I discuss the specifics on how to do this in the next chapter, but trust me when I say you need to address any issues with attitude and interest in order to have a successful year.

You'll also record any observations about interest and stamina during the pre-assessment. Take note of how many students write for a few minutes and then run out of ideas or get distracted. You may find that this is an issue for your entire group, or it may be just a few individual students. I share a fantastic writing stamina activity in the next chapter to help either a whole group or small group of students increase their stamina before you start your first unit.

Observations to Record before, during, and after Writing Pre-Assessment		
Before Pre-Assessment *Interest and Stamina*	**During Pre-Assessment** *Interest and Stamina, Technology*	**When Reviewing Submitted Samples** *Technical Skills*
• Students resistant to or excited about writing time • Students requiring discussion or other supports in order to begin	• Writing for a short amount of time (lack of writing stamina) • Unable to write independently without the teacher's help • Struggling with technology (if applicable)	• Inability to write complete sentences or organized paragraphs • Lack of complex ideas • Gaps in writing structure • Grammar and spelling issues • Other major gaps in skills

After the five days of pre-assessment are complete, you will review students' submitted samples and record data on technical skills in your spreadsheet. Set aside two to three hours to review samples and record this data. Remember that the purpose is not to grade on a rubric, make corrections on the paper, or give specific feedback to them. You should spend about 5–10 minutes on each set of student samples, recording their individual skills and making a note of whole group issues you see repeatedly.

I know this can seem time-consuming with everything you have on your plate, but this one-time activity of analyzing and recording their writing pieces will give you important data that you will use throughout the year. This information will help you tailor your lessons to the needs of your students as well as set up small groups and focused conferences to fill in individual learning gaps. Because you will use this information to tweak your lessons, you will have more lightbulb moments sooner instead of seeing your students make the same mistakes over and over again because you can't pinpoint the skills they're missing.

RECORDING IMPORTANT WHOLE GROUP SKILLS

The whole group tab of your spreadsheet (see Table 5.1) will give a general overview of where your students struggle as a group. It provides a quick pulse on your classroom. Namely, observing and recording "big picture" items like stamina, interests, and attitude toward writing will help you prepare your students and yourself for upcoming units. By filling in this part of the spreadsheet, there will be very few surprises when you get to your first unit. You'll also be able to frontload some of these skills with simple lessons from the next chapter.

Table 5.1

Interest & Stamina	Sentence Writing	Paragraph Writing	Complexity of Ideas
Students seemed interested before writing began, but they were a little hesitant to write independently. Discussion did help encourage them to come up with ideas for the prompt. Stamina was a struggle. I had to continue to remind students to keep writing.	Most students wrote complete sentences with punctuation.	80% of students struggled with paragraph structure.	Students struggled to provide facts to support their informational and opinion writing. Narrative writing lacked description and character development.
What this means for my whole group instruction: My students get their ideas flowing with discussion, so I will include more of that. I'm going to teach students about stamina next week and make that a big focus in our future units.	**What this means for my whole group instruction:** There were only a few students who struggled to write complete sentences, so I can provide them with sentence frames during our whole group instruction and work with them in small groups, in the future. I do not need to make sentence writing a big focus in our upcoming lessons.	**What this means for my whole group instruction:** Most of my students struggle with paragraph structure, which is an important skill they need to master in order to independently write during our upcoming units. I need to review paragraph writing before we get into our on-grade-level units, and I need to model it thoroughly in upcoming writing lessons.	**What this means for my whole group instruction:** I will need to build in more idea generation opportunities and discussion into future units by using structured discussion, research, and simple graphic organizers.

(continued)

Table 5.1 *(continued)*

Technology Knowledge	Other: Elements of Narrative	Other: Informational Structure
Most students were able to open the shared file in Google Classroom without issue. They were able to use most Google Doc tools that we would use during writing time. Typing was very slow.	Most students did not use narrative structure properly, including dialogue. The few that used dialogue had trouble properly formatting and punctuating it. Setting development was missing. Strong endings were also a struggle.	Students struggled to transition from one paragraph to the next. They needed extra help on supporting ideas with reason and evidence.
What this means for my whole group instruction: My students need extra time to practice typing.	**What this means for my whole group instruction:** I will need to focus on all aspects of narrative structure and add additional lessons for dialogue.	**What this means for my whole group instruction:** I need to add additional lessons and practice opportunities for transitions. I need to focus on supporting ideas with reasons and evidence in multiple steps of the writing process.

"BIG PICTURE" SKILLS: INTEREST AND WRITING STAMINA

Interest & Stamina
Students seemed interested before writing began, but they were a little hesitant to write independently. Discussion did help encourage them to come up with ideas for the prompt. Stamina was a struggle. I had to continue to remind students to keep writing.
What this means for my whole group instruction: My students get their ideas flowing with discussion, so I will include more of that. I'm going to teach students about stamina next week and make that a big focus in our future units. *See Chapter 6 for my writing stamina lesson.*

In my whole group recording, I noted that students seemed interested in the prompt, but a bit hesitant to start on their own. However, a little bit of class discussion made it easier for them to get started on their own writing. It may seem a bit counterintuitive to some to intervene at all during a pre-assessment, but I see this time as an opportunity to identify if there's something simple that works for their struggle. Now, going into future units, I can utilize discussion to support their independent writing. I encourage you to explore simple ways to help your students start writing, while taking notes on what works (and what doesn't).

Discussion Strategies:
- Share your own response to the prompt and allow them to ask you questions so that you can expand upon your response.
- Write a sentence starter on the board to help them create their first sentence for the prompt. For example, "My best day ever was the day I _____."

- Have your students share a verbal response with a partner and then have the partner ask them questions about it.
- Provide your students with one or more questions to ask their partner about the prompt. For example, "Ask your partner to tell you what their favorite movie is and to retell it using only five sentences with the most important parts. Use your hand to count the sentences as you talk when it's your turn."

If you notice that students are confused or lack engagement with the prompt and discussion doesn't help, it's worth getting students' input and changing the prompt. Remember that your goal is to learn about them as writers. Providing support during a pre-assessment may be frowned upon if you're merely trying to get pre-and-post scores, but the purpose of our writing pre-assessment is learning everything we can about our students' approach to writing to better support them.

One major thing I noticed for our whole group recording was that students rushed to get their writing done as quickly as possible. Many students stopped writing around the five- to seven-minute mark. I had allotted about 25 minutes for this response, but no one used the entire time to write. This tells me that the students struggle with writing stamina as a group, and it's something I'll absolutely address before moving into our regular units.

SENTENCE AND PARAGRAPH WRITING

Sentence Writing	Paragraph Writing
Most students wrote complete sentences with punctuation.	80% of students struggled with paragraph structure.
What this means for my whole group instruction: There were only a few students who struggled to write complete sentences, so I can provide them sentence frames during our whole group instruction and work with them in small groups in the future. I do not need to make sentence writing a big focus in our upcoming lessons.	**What this means for my whole group instruction:** Most of my students struggle with paragraph structure, which is an important skill they need to master in order to independently write during our upcoming units. I need to review paragraph writing before we get into our on-grade-level units, and I need to model it thoroughly in upcoming writing lessons.

It's expected for students in third grade and up to be able to write full sentences and paragraphs. The reality is that mastery of this skill is not always there, even in middle and high school. This is why sentence and paragraph writing are important skills to observe when reviewing your completed student samples.

You may be wondering why this is included on both the whole group and individual tab. Remember that the general overview of your class's "big picture" ideas and foundational skills will help immensely when you're planning your whole group lessons. If only a few students struggle with paragraph writing, you won't need a lot of additional whole group lessons for that skill in your regular units. If 80% of your students struggle with paragraph writing, you won't be able to teach your on-grade-level lesson without special support in place.

Common sentence-writing struggles to look for:
- Incomplete sentences/unfinished ideas
- Difficulty with sentence structure or word order

- Awkward grammar
- Lack of sentence variety (simple, compound, and complex)

Common paragraph-writing struggles to look for:
- No topic or concluding sentence
- Missing evidence or elaboration
- Off-topic information that doesn't match the main idea
- Information isn't organized into correct paragraphs
- Lack of transitions between paragraphs

COMPLEXITY OF IDEAS

Complexity of Ideas
Students struggled to provide facts to support their informational and opinion writing. Narrative writing lacked description and character development.
What this means for my whole group instruction: I will need to build in more idea generation opportunities and discussion in future units by using structured discussion, research, and simple graphic organizers.

The next skill I'm looking for in completed student work is complexity of ideas, the ability for students to develop their ideas using complex thoughts, facts, and evidence. A closely related skill you may be more familiar with is elaboration, which helps develop the writing piece by supporting the student's ideas and providing important details for the reader. Complexity of ideas is an element that is often overlooked because there are so many obvious structural and grammatical mistakes, but it can often be the difference between good and great writing pieces.

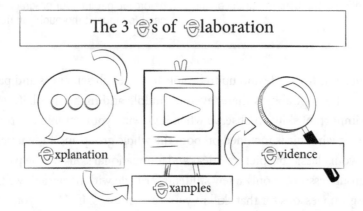

The 3 e's of elaboration

explanation   examples   evidence

If your students can't put together sentences and paragraphs, it's very likely that they will also struggle to include complex ideas that build off each other. In my example, students struggled to even provide facts to support their ideas, leaving them with mostly basic, unsupported ideas in their writing. It was no surprise that they also struggled with description and character development in their narrative writing because elaboration is one of the class's major skill gaps.

Turn your attention to how your class develops ideas in their writing samples. This skill can look very different in each writing piece, so I've given a few examples of specific issues to look for. If you're seeing all of these examples and more, don't panic. There are simple ways to build extra support for idea generation and elaboration into your upcoming units. The more confident your students become as writers throughout the year, the more you'll be able to focus on adding more complex ideas to their writing.

What to look for in informational/opinion writing:
- No detailed planning organizer
- No elaboration given on the important topics or opinions
- Repetitive ideas
- Basic facts instead of complex ideas that build upon each other

What to look for in narrative writing:
- Not describing the setting
- Lack of character development
- Dialogue shows basic, not complex, thoughts (or they did not use dialogue at all)
- Basic story structure that's missing plot elements
- Missing important context for the readers

You may notice that your students who have mastered the basic grammatical and structural skills in their writing elaborate more and include some complex ideas. When we get to recording individual skills, this category will be a place for growth for these students who are at or above grade level and ready for more. When I taught gifted learners and high achievers, I found myself focusing a lot of my attention on complexity of ideas. A good deal of my energy went to helping them organize all their ideas so that they built off each other and provided a more multifaceted overview of the topic.

TECHNOLOGY KNOWLEDGE

Technology Knowledge
Most students were able to open the shared file in Google Classroom without issue. They were able to use most Google Doc tools that we would use during writing time. Typing was very slow.
What this means for my whole group instruction: My students need extra time to practice typing.

If your students will be using a computer or other device for their writing, it's important to record any issues that you observe during the pre-assessment. This means you should conduct your pre-assessment using the same tools your students will use during writing time. For most classrooms, this also involves the use of an e-learning platform and a keyboard.

Take note of any procedures your students struggle with on your e-learning platform. Some examples of common technology struggles are locating assignments, editing documents, and turning in work. You'll need extra time to go over these procedures before your first unit, and you'll likely need to build in a few extra minutes during the initial units to practice these new technology skills.

Another common issue you may see is slow or inaccurate typing. If your students struggle to write because they are slowed down by typing, you will need to help them strengthen their typing skills to support their independent writing. I often notice that students can use the tools to correct their spelling and other mistakes, but their typing is so inaccurate that they have to spend a lot of time doing so. It may seem like an additional time-consuming task, but it will save you time in the long run to take the time to practice efficient and accurate typing.

OTHER WHOLE GROUP CATEGORIES

There are a few extra columns on your pre-assessment recording sheet for any other details you need to make note of. Don't get bogged down adding so many minute skills and details to the spreadsheet. This will cause data fatigue and make it harder for you to focus on the "big picture" foundational skills that matter the most. The best use of the "other" column is for glaring issues that need to be addressed soon or need modification plans for your upcoming units.

If you want to include information on what you saw the class struggle with on the different writing types, you can use those columns for that purpose like I do in my example. I refer to this spreadsheet when planning each of my units, so it's helpful to have a quick reminder of what lessons I may need to expand when planning my first units.

Narrative	Informational/Opinion Elements
Most students did not use narrative structure properly, including dialogue. The few that used dialogue had trouble properly formatting and punctuating it. Setting development was missing. Strong endings were also a struggle.	Students struggled transitioning from one paragraph to the next. They need extra help on supporting ideas with reason and evidence.
What this means for my whole group instruction: I will need to focus on all aspects of narrative structure and add additional lessons for dialogue.	**What this means for my whole group instruction:** I need to add in additional lessons and practice opportunities for transitions. I need to focus on supporting ideas with reason and evidence in multiple steps of the writing process.

WHAT THIS MEANS FOR MY WHOLE GROUP INSTRUCTION

The pre-assessment and recording alone won't make much of a difference in your writing block. What you actually *do* with this information throughout the year is what will help your writers grow. This is why I've included a "What This Means for My Whole Group Instruction" section on the spreadsheet. This section is where you will write how you are going to take action on this information. Some of these actions may take place immediately, while other items will be built into your upcoming units as needed.

In the next two chapters, I give you specific strategies to use to address the issues that you note on the whole group sheet. These strategies will not only help you create a classroom climate conducive to writing, but they will also help you mold your current writing units to better fit the needs of your students. Taking action on this data using these strategies is the best way to set up your students for success, while making your lessons less stressful for you to plan and implement.

WHOLE GROUP GRAMMAR KNOCK-OUT LIST

You may have noticed that grammar is missing from the whole group summary page. The reason for this is that we know students will struggle with many different grammatical concepts. Although many states have grade-level grammar standards, you'll find yourself reteaching a lot of skills that students struggle with year after year. You'll see a lot of improvement in student writing if you can help students finally master certain key grammar skills.

There are two ways to fill in this part of the spreadsheet (Table 5.2). You can either create a running list on a sticky note of grammatical errors you see repeatedly in student samples, or you can create your list from looking at which concepts most students struggled with on the individual tab. If more than 60% of your class struggles with a concept, it's worth noting it on this spreadsheet.

Table 5.2

Grammar Skill	When will this unit be taught?	Date the unit was completed:	Notes:
List the grammar skills you need to cover from greatest impact to least impact and add notes as you cover each skill.			
End Punctuation	Week of 8/15	8-19	Most students scored 85% or above, updated on individual tab
Capitalization	Week of 8/22	8-26	Pull small groups to review capitalizing proper nouns
Fragments & Run-Ons	Week of 8/29	9-2	May need to reteach in small groups (Dahlia, Savannah, Julian)
Subject-Verb Agreement	Week of 9/6	9-9	Average score 82%, continue to review as needed
Compound Sentences	Week of 9/12		
Complex Sentences	Week of 9/19		
Dialogue Punctuation	Week of 9/26		
Comma Usage	Week of 10/3		
Titles of Works	Week of 10/10		
Quotation Marks	Week of 10/17		
Verb Tense	Week of 10/24		
Pronouns	Week of 10/31		
Quoting Text	Week of 11/7		

Sequence will differ from one class to the next.

THE ORDER MATTERS

The order you list grammar concepts on this spreadsheet is important. Instead of listing it by most common error to least common error, consider which errors cause the biggest disruption in readability. For example, fragments and run-ons are common issues that interrupt readability. The same could be said for punctuation. Put at the top the skills where you would see the biggest impact in writing pieces if your students mastered them, then prioritize from most important to least important.

This part of the spreadsheet will dictate what grammar lessons you focus on as a whole group throughout the year. If less than 60% of your students are struggling with a concept, you can leave that to the individual section of the spreadsheet. You will learn more about how to fit these concepts into your whole group and small group lessons in Part IV. For now, focus on getting the data you need to identify which gaps you'll be filling in throughout the year.

RECORDING INDIVIDUAL SKILLS

Imagine if you could help every student increase their writing ability, no matter how far behind grade level they are. This can be done, if you have the proper data organized in a way you can *actually* use. Having access to a list of the gaps in writing skills for each individual student (Table 5.3) is a tool you may not have known you needed, but you will never want to be without again. This list tells you exactly which gaps you need to fill in for individual students to improve their writing ability. Beginning in Quarter 2, when you feel confident with your instruction, you'll be able to refer to the spreadsheet to form small groups around individual skills.

I like to keep my recording simple, so on my sample spreadsheet I used an asterisk to note that a student struggled with the concept. This is a fast way to record for each individual student as you review their samples. Remember that you're looking for patterns that show a gap in knowledge, so something like a single misuse of punctuation is not worth recording.

For conventions, I only note the highest priority grammar and spelling issues. This can be a long laundry list of skills for some students, so limit what you record to the mistakes you see the most in their writing.

Table 5.3

Student Names	Stamina	Sentence Writing	Paragraph Writing	Complexity of Ideas	Grammar & Spelling (Highest Priority)
Enter student names and mark categories where the student struggles with an X. List specific grammar skills in that column.ww					
Abdias	x			x	dialogue punctuation
Bryce	x		x	x	punctuation, spelling
Brynn	x		x	x	short, choppy sentences, verb tense
Carlos					spelling
Chantelle	x		x	x	capitalization of proper nouns, spelling
Dahlia			x		run-on sentences, punctuation
Dara					pronoun clarity
Ethan					
Evelina	x		x	x	capitalization, short sentences
Ezra	x		x	x	end punctuation, spelling
Genesis	x		x	x	using quotation marks
Grace					
Isaiah	x	x	x	x	punctuation, spelling, capitalization
Jackson	x		x	x	capitalizing titles of works, spelling
Jayden					
Julian	x		x	x	subject-verb agreement, some run-ons
Kevin	x		x	x	commas, quotation marks, spelling

Student Names	Stamina	Sentence Writing	Paragraph Writing	Complexity of Ideas	Grammar & Spelling (Highest Priority)
Madelynn			x		dialogue punctuation
McKynna	x		x	x	capitalization, dialogue punctuation, verb tense
Nicholas					verb tense, spelling
Olivia	x			x	quoting text - punctuation
Rowan	x		x	x	sentence fragments, capitalization, spelling
Sanjay					comma usage, pronoun use
Savannah	x	x	x	x	fragments & run-on sentences, end punctuation
Sharae	x			x	comma usage, some run-ons/fragments
Sophia				x	comma usage
Trevor	x	x	x	x	subject-verb agreement, spelling
Uriel	x		x		run-ons, beginning capitalization
Xochitl					spelling

SETTING GOALS AND RECORDING SUCCESS

The individual student sheet is the best place to note areas of growth for each student. This can be very helpful when the time comes to prepare grades or write report card comments. You may have many students not writing at grade level, but adding a comment about the skills they've mastered during the quarter is a helpful way to let the student and their guardians know that they're making progress. If a student has been repeatedly working on a skill in small group or as an individual goal after conferring with you, and you notice that they've mastered it in their writing piece, make a note of it!

For students who have very few issues marked (or none), the "other" columns on the sheet can be a helpful place to add above-grade-level skills. You can also convert these columns to a place for notes where you can add areas of challenge for these students, such as higher-level vocabulary and research.

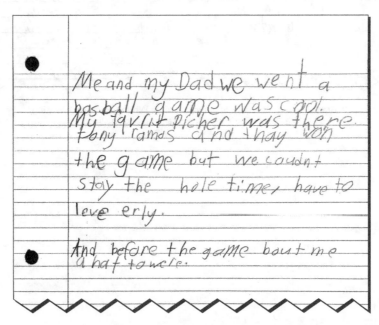

3rd Grade Sample | Concerns: Stamina, Sentence Writing, Paragraph Formatting, Complexity of Ideas, Punctuation, Spelling, and Capitalization.

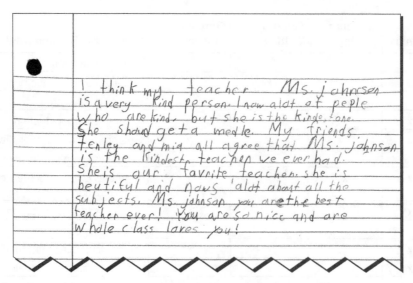

I think my teacher Ms. johnson is a very kind person. I now a lot of peple who are kind, but she is the kinde one. She shoud get a medle. My friends tenley and mia all agree that Ms. johnson is the kindest teacher we ever had. She is our favrite teacher. she is beutiful and nows 'a lot about all the subjects. Ms. johnson you are the best teacher ever! You are so nice and are whole class loves you!

4th Grade Sample | Concerns: Stamina, Paragraph Writing, Complexity of Ideas, Punctuation, Spelling, and Capitalization of Proper Nouns.

Yes they should. Some kids uses a lot of screen time, some not so much. But its up to parents to decide if there kids should. So they should limitting it to like 2 hours a day. They can watch a little TV and use there phone but then needs to turn it off. Or if they are doing something educatonal for school thats okay. Need to have a limitt so they don't uses it too much.

6th Grade Sample | Concerns: Stamina, Sentence Writing, Paragraph Writing, Fragments, Subject-Verb Agreement, and Spelling.

Seattle is a popular place to visit. It's one of my favorite vacation spots. Located in northwest Washington. There are a lot of interesting and unique things to do in Seattle so, many tourists travel there every year.

One of the most popular places to visit in Seattle is Pike Place Market. There are a lot of shops where you can go shopping. They also have a fish market, they sell fresh seafood. So visitors can go shopping and eat seafood at the restaurants. They have shrimp, lobster, and all different kinds of seafood to try. I love shopping there with my mom everytime we visit. We always get shrimp for dinner when we go to the Pike Place Market.

Tourists can also visit the Space Needle in Seattle. This is a really tall building where you can look out over the whole town. There is an elevator so, you don't have to walk up the stairs if you don't want to. The Space Needle has an observation deck you will have a great view of the entire city. It is the highest building in Seattle.

In conclusion, Seattle is a great place to visit.

7th Grade Sample | Concerns: Complexity of Ideas, Comma Usage, Run-on Sentences, and Conclusion.

After you have the pre-assessment spreadsheet filled in, you may feel daunted to think about tackling every skill gap that your students have. Remember that you will not be able to address every single issue. The most important thing is that you use this data to help your students fill in the most important gaps while teaching your on-grade-level lessons. This will help you finally get out of the loop of teaching your whole group lessons and getting student pieces with the same exact issues.

Remember that every writing skill your students master or improve upon is a boost to their overall writing ability. That may not bring all your students to grade level, but it will help them communicate better in all subject areas. In upcoming chapters, I teach you exactly how to use this data to move the needle on some of the toughest skill gaps. All of these simple strategies will be easy to build into your current writing block; no complicated activities are necessary.

Reflect and Plan

Download a copy of the recording spreadsheet and put it somewhere easy to access on your computer. When will you record the information from your student samples? Put it on your calendar so that the time is set aside for this important activity. What are you excited about the most when it comes to having this specific data?

CHAPTER 6

Build a Foundation

When glancing at your pre-assessment recording spreadsheet, it may seem like you have an uphill battle ahead of you. When I looked at my first set of data, I was completely overwhelmed by how many key writing skills my students were missing. It wasn't until a few months into the process that I realized how fulfilling it was for me to see them growing in different areas instead of constantly pulling my hair out expecting them all to work on grade level.

The first week or two after your pre-assessment are all about prepping students for success by filling in foundational issues. You may be tempted to go straight into your writing unit next, especially with the limited time you have. I urge you to look at your spreadsheet to determine if there are any major issues that will impact your class's ability to tackle that first unit. In most classes, we see at least one major issue that will make an on-grade level lesson more of a struggle than it needs to be. Addressing these issues before moving on to your first unit will make a huge difference in how smoothly your lessons go.

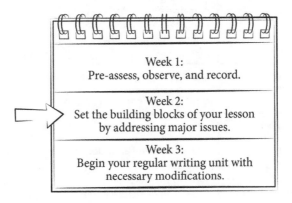

Your students may not be ready for grade level writing instruction, but there are a few foundational skills you can introduce and practice to better prepare them for your lessons. As a part of this chapter, I have a few fantastic lessons for you to use if your class needs them. **There's no need to use all the lessons. You'll pick and choose based off what your class needs the most as a group.** We discuss how to tackle these issues with individuals or small groups of students in Chapter 12, which covers differentiation and small group.

Foundational Issues	Issues to Address in Your Regular Units
Attitude Toward Writing/Lack of Interest	Grammar
Writing Stamina	Spelling
Sentence or Paragraph Writing	Organization/Staying on Topic
Idea Generation	Word Choice

To choose which foundational lessons you will teach, you'll need your calendar and your pre-assessment spreadsheet. It's important to tailor this to your class's unique needs, choosing the most pressing issues first. If most of your students can't start writing, you'll need to prioritize idea generation before stamina. If your students are close to mastering paragraph writing, you can spend less time on those lessons.

Foundational Issues My Class Struggles
with, In Order of Severity:

-Idea Generation

-Writing Stamina

-Paragraph Writing (Almost Mastered)

-Attitude Toward Writing

Foundational Week 1 Example				
Monday	**Tuesday**	**Wednesday**	**Thursday**	**Friday**
Give *Generating Ideas* mini-lesson.	Give *Piggybacking* mini-lesson.	Cut & organize personal narrative discussion questions; talk about how we will use these to generate ideas.	Generate ideas for personal narrative on the *Make a List* page.	Practice using the personal narrative discussion questions and idea list to journal about a chosen topic.
Start showing students how to use Sticky Notes, fun pens, and flexible writing areas.				

Foundational Week 2 Example				
Monday	**Tuesday**	**Wednesday**	**Thursday**	**Friday**
Give *Writing Stamina* mini-lesson. Practice with visual prompt #1.	Practice with visual prompt #2. Cut strips and have students randomly choose one for practice #3.	Give *Parts of a Paragraph* mini-lesson. Practice highlighting the parts on the *Paragraph Structure* page.	Use *Build a Paragraph* and *Cross It Off!* pages in groups.	Practice writing paragraphs and record stamina on graph.
Continue to practice procedures for fun supplies and flexible writing areas.				

The foundational lessons listed are all included in the downloadable book resources. Notice how I didn't include every concept from this chapter, or even every lesson from the units I prioritized. It's important to balance what your students struggle with the most with the amount of time you have. I included a lot of extra lessons for each topic in case you have more time or your whole class only struggles with one foundational concept. You can use any extra lesson in future small group lessons if you have only a handful of students who struggle with the concept.

Chapter 5 discusses these foundational issues and how to record any whole group patterns that you notice. In that chapter, I also show a few examples of how to set a basic plan to address foundational issues in the "What this means for my whole group instruction" section of your spreadsheet. Now, we'll actually put this into action by choosing the most glaring foundational issues that your class has and using targeted lessons to help build the foundation and prepare them for upcoming units.

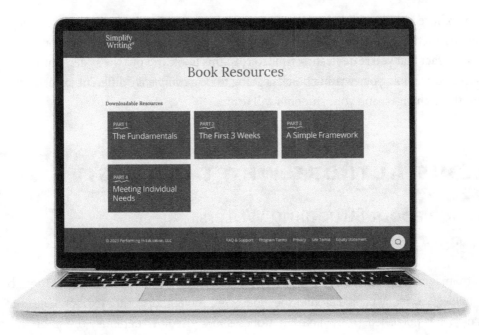

There's no need to recreate the organizers in this section. The link icon (⊚) means there is a download-able resource available that goes with the chapter. You can create a free account and access these resources by visiting: https://www.simplifywriting.com/book-resources.

INTEREST AND ATTITUDE

With how challenging writing can be for students, it's no surprise that many feel discouraged when start-ing a writing assignment. Many upper-elementary and middle school students have experienced years of frustration with writing. We unknowingly set them up for failure when we rush our lessons and don't have a dedicated writing time to properly support them. Although you can't undo that damage, you have the opportunity to start this year fresh and show them just how enjoyable it can be to write in your classroom.

ADDRESSING YOUR OWN WRITING BAGGAGE

A memory comes to mind every time I think about my writing experiences in school: I was in 6th grade, sitting in the cafeteria with my folder up and taking state ELA test. I was rocking this test, answering the multiple-choice questions about the provided text like it was nothing. I was an avid reader, often reading books several grade levels above. Then, I got to a section with lined paper and a single creative writing prompt. I froze. I had read hundreds of books already, but I couldn't come up with one single idea that seemed anywhere near what these authors had written. My perfectionism kicked in, leaving me paralyzed and unable to complete the assignment.

Your baggage can either get in the way of your writing instruction or it can augment it. Teachers often feel like they need to seem like the expert at everything in front of their students, but this is far from the truth. A simple way to improve your students' attitude toward writing is by being open and honest about your own struggles.

You may also have past baggage when it comes to teaching writing. As you read in the beginning of the book, writing instruction challenges are all too common. It's important to realize that you are not a bad writing teaching. The fact that you're dedicating time to read this book and put the system into place proves that. With the tools in this book, your writing block is going to be a *completely* different experience this year. Get excited about these changes, and your students will too!

FAMOUS AUTHORS WHO DIDN'T GIVE UP

A Passage about Struggling Writers

By Rachel Peachey

It's hard to imagine any publisher rejecting famous books like *Dune* or *Harry Potter*. These books are classics, beloved by many people around the world. Yet, the authors of these books and many others struggled to get published. Their amazing stories show just how determined authors need to be to succeed.

Dune, by Frank Herbert, is a famous science-fiction novel that has now been made into a movie. However, Herbert received rejection letters from 23 different publishers. Even after all that, Herbert's novel was accepted by Chilton Books. This publisher usually published car manuals. Despite all that, *Dune* eventually grew popular and even won important awards! Today, it remains the best-selling science fiction novel of all time.

Similarly, J.K. Rowling's first Harry Potter book was rejected 12 times. When she found a publisher for the book, the editor wasn't enthusiastic. He wasn't convinced the book would achieve much success. Today, the series has broken many world records. *The Deathly Hallows* earned the title of most books printed in the first printing with 12 million copies. Despite this great success, J.K. Rowling has still experienced rejection. Using a pen name, she sent off a mystery novel to various publishers who rejected it. Finally, *The Cuckoo's Calling* was published, becoming a series of its own!

The famous novel *Little Women* also got a rough start. In one of her rejection letters, Louisa May Alcott was reportedly told to "Stick to teaching. . .you can't write." Thankfully, Alcott didn't give up and found a publisher for the book. First published in 1868, *Little Women* is still a popular novel today that has even been made into a movie. Alcott also went on to write many more books, including a few sequels to *Little Women*.

Yet another author who experienced rejection is Agatha Christie. Today, she is known for her 65 detective novels and 14 short-story collections. Christie is easily one of the world's most famous mystery writers. Yet, her first novel was never even published. However, in one rejection letter, the agent suggested that Christie try writing another novel. After more rejection, the novel was finally published, giving her the start she needed as an author. Christie's books are so popular they've been translated into over 100 languages.

Despite many rejections and difficulties along the way, great authors don't give up. Thanks to their persistence and determination, we can now enjoy reading their books today! These famous authors also set an important example for hopeful writers. With their example, they teach upcoming writers to keep working toward their goals even when things are tough.

If you don't have struggles to share, you can tell your students about the many ways that famous authors have struggled over the years. Not only have many authors shared that they've had manuscripts turned down repeatedly, but a few have even shared report cards showing poor marks or comments about their writing abilities. The passage "Famous Authors Who Didn't Give Up" is a great way to open the discussion about failure and perseverance. You can find this resource in the downloadable files in the Appendix.

File 6.0 Famous Authors' Rejection Passage

CULTIVATING A POSITIVE CLASSROOM ENVIRONMENT

In addition to being open and honest about how normal it is to struggle with writing, there are many ways you can show how fun writing can be. These beginning weeks are the best time to start adding novelty to your writing block to set it apart from the other subjects. I'm not saying that you shouldn't make every subject fun, but making writing special in simple ways can encourage students to relax and enjoy it more.

There's no need for an additional lesson here. Simply start incorporating a few of the following ideas into your writing time during the foundational lessons you choose. You can also come back to this list for future units if it feels like things are getting stale or any of the ideas aren't working for your classroom.

- Make writing a "judgment-free zone."
- Get excited about teaching writing.
- Use fun supplies like colored pencils, sticky notes, and highlighters.
- Allow students to write somewhere other than their desks.
- Take your lessons to the carpet.
- Have students walk around to generate ideas with others.
- Give students time to illustrate ideas.
- Have students record themselves reading their writing aloud.
- Allow students to share their writing with the class or a small group.
- Publish writing in the classroom or online for others to read.
- Connect books, movies, TV shows, or current events to writing.
- Celebrate works in progress, not perfection.

Any idea that brings novelty to your writing block, without creating a huge distraction, can be a great way to get your students excited about writing. Just remember that anything you do should be simple and easy to manage. If you can't sustain it every day, it's not the best choice. If you find that any of the ideas you choose are creating a headache for you, it's perfectly fine to try something different that's a better fit for your class.

One day, I decided to fill some extra time at the end of class by allowing a strong writer to share their work under the doc camera. The class was so engaged praising the student's writing. The next day, I announced at the beginning of the lesson that we would have some time to share at the end, and one of my struggling writers in particular was very motivated to be chosen to share. Although his writing that day was not very promising, I allowed him to share anyways. The rest of the class was so encouraging, offering positive comments and suggestions for improvement as well. This student didn't typically get the spotlight, so having the whole class focus on him was new. I started making this sharing time a priority, and using it to especially encourage students who were feeling less than motivated. It made a huge difference in their attitudes toward writing and they really began to look forward to that part of the writing workshop.

– Laura Jones, 6th-Grade Teacher

My writing block takes place right after lunch. It can be challenging to reengage students as they come in off the playground, especially in a subject like writing where many students often struggle. I started to try out a few new strategies to help get my students excited about writing after lunch. One thing that worked well was having a special set of class gel pens just for our writing block. All of my students were so excited to choose their gel pen for the day and get started with their writing assignments. The gel pens were pretty cheap for a bulk set on Amazon and 100% worth the payoff I got in student engagement and excitement.

– Myranda McDonald, 3rd-Grade Teacher

WRITING STAMINA

Writing stamina is a commonly overlooked area where students struggle. There's a variety of reasons why students have poor stamina. For many, it's simply a matter of not having the time to write in past years. If you've found yourself teaching a whole group lesson that goes off the rails and doesn't allow for more than five minutes of student writing time, that can be a contributor to the stamina issue. Students are trained to rush to finish, which leads to less discussion, elaboration, and complex thoughts.

We need to help our students reverse the bad habit of rushing to get done. Part of this means setting a schedule that allows for them to have a comfortable amount of time to write. The other part is creating better habits by teaching them about writing stamina and practicing these new behaviors. This is where the writing stamina unit comes in. If most of your class has good writing stamina already, you can skip this lesson and focus on the foundational issue(s) they really need.

🔗 D6.1 Writing Stamina Lesson

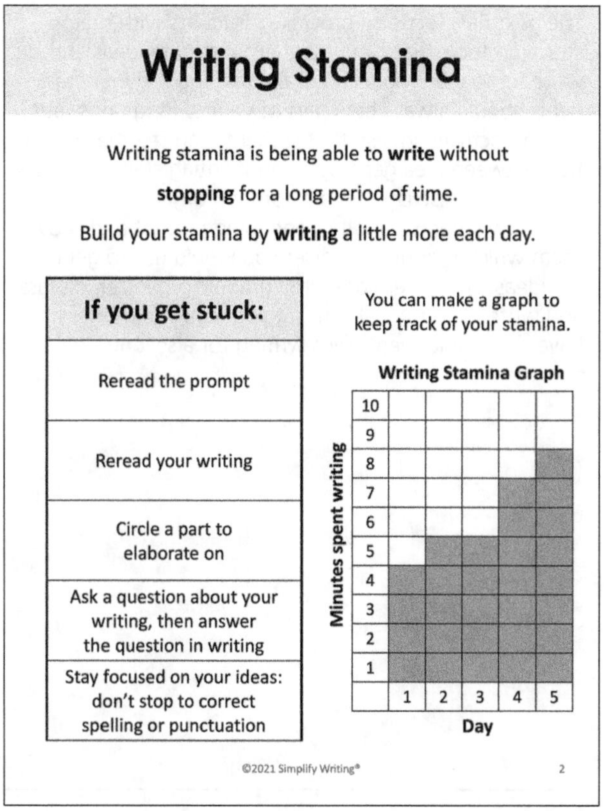

Writing Stamina

Writing stamina is being able to **write** without

stopping for a long period of time.

Build your stamina by **writing** a little more each day.

If you get stuck:
Reread the prompt
Reread your writing
Circle a part to elaborate on
Ask a question about your writing, then answer the question in writing
Stay focused on your ideas: don't stop to correct spelling or punctuation

You can make a graph to keep track of your stamina.

Writing Stamina Graph

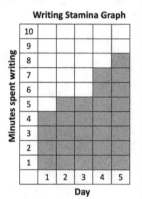

Minutes spent writing / Day

©2021 Simplify Writing®   2

Day 1: Introduce Writing Stamina

Use the writing stamina anchor chart to teach students what stamina is and why it's important. I've included a student copy so that they can take notes and keep this in their writing binder/folder for future writing assignments. Take the time to discuss times when real writers must have stamina (finishing an article for a deadline, reporting daily news, writing a chapter in a book) and how we can use the same behaviors they do to create more comprehensive writing pieces. Then, discuss what students can do if they get stuck. The anchor chart includes some great ideas, but you're more than welcome to add more!

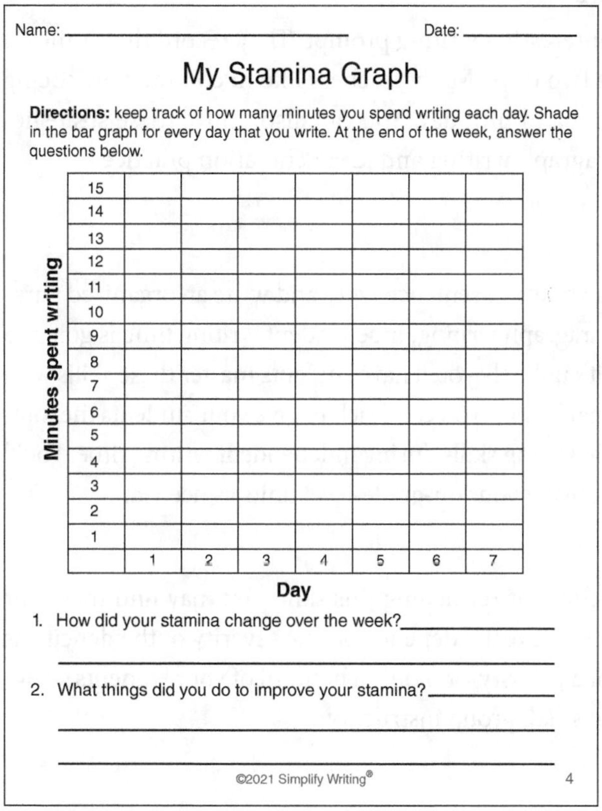

Name: _____   Date: _____

My Stamina Graph

Directions: keep track of how many minutes you spend writing each day. Shade in the bar graph for every day that you write. At the end of the week, answer the questions below.

Minutes spent writing (vertical axis: 1–15) / Day (horizontal axis: 1–7)

1. How did your stamina change over the week? _____

_____

2. What things did you do to improve your stamina? _____

_____

_____

©2021 Simplify Writing®   4

It can be difficult for students to gauge how much time they're working on their writing. This is especially true if students have been trained to rush to complete a writing piece. A graph is a simple way to track their daily stamina throughout this practice week and in future lessons. After you're done teaching about what writing stamina is, have students practice it using the stamina graph and an engaging journaling prompt. I like to display a count-up timer, which you can find for free online, so that students can write down the time it's at on their paper when they finish journaling.

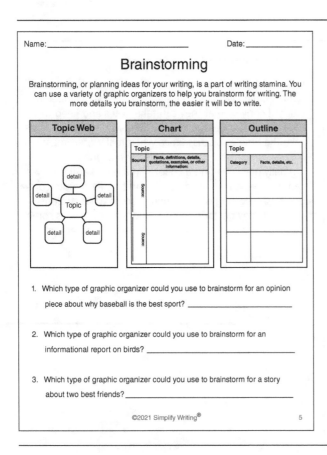

Name: _____ Date: _____

Brainstorming

Brainstorming, or planning ideas for your writing, is a part of writing stamina. You can use a variety of graphic organizers to help you brainstorm for writing. The more details you brainstorm, the easier it will be to write.

Topic Web

Chart

Outline

1. Which type of graphic organizer could you use to brainstorm for an opinion piece about why baseball is the best sport? _____

2. Which type of graphic organizer could you use to brainstorm for an informational report on birds? _____

3. Which type of graphic organizer could you use to brainstorm for a story about two best friends? _____

©2021 Simplify Writing®   5

Day 2: Provide Brainstorming Tools

The next day, focus on providing students with brainstorming tools that can help them generate ideas and write for longer. Modeling brainstorming for your students should always be a part of your writing units, but I use this activity now so that students can see the connection between idea generation and writing stamina. When you're done discussing brainstorming organization, you can show students another engaging prompt and show them which graphic organizer you would use to generate ideas. Have them draw the graphic organizer, discuss, and write ideas on it. Then, set your count-up timer and have them time themselves writing for a second time.

DAYS 3–5: PRACTICE, PRACTICE, PRACTICE

On Day 3, have students continue to journal using an interesting writing prompt. They record their time on their stamina graph and utilize the tools from the first two days. Many teachers like to continue practicing the entire week, so feel free to keep it going for a fourth and fifth day. You can also utilize these strategies while working on other foundational concepts like paragraph writing and idea generation practice.

SENTENCE AND PARAGRAPH WRITING

Students in 3rd grade and above should be able to form a variety of sentence types and write an organized paragraph. If most of your class struggles with sentence or paragraph writing, independent writing time is going to be a challenge without reteaching these skills. Although it's unlikely you'll have students master these skills with just a few days of instruction, there are several foundational lessons you can teach to give your students the tools they need to continue to practice sentence and paragraph writing skills during independent writing time. You'll continue to work on sentence and/or paragraph writing during your on-grade-level units as needed.

Sentence Writing Intervention

This activity includes five days of sentence writing practice for reteaching this skill. You may find that your students pick it up quickly and don't need all the activities. It really depends on the severity of the deficit. As with the other foundational issues, skip this one if it's not a priority, or if only a handful of your students struggle with it. You can always use these lessons later during small group instruction.

◎ D6.2 Complete Sentence Lesson

Complete Sentences

A complete sentence needs a **subject** and a **predicate**.

Subject	Predicate
<u>who</u> or <u>what</u> the sentence is about	what the subject <u>does</u> or <u>is</u> (starts with or contains a verb)

<u>The boy</u> walked to the store.

<u>Mr. and Mrs. Jones</u> went on a picnic.

<u>The principal of our school</u> is home sick.

<u>Check to make sure your sentence:</u>

❑ has a subject and predicate

❑ begins with a capital letter

❑ ends with the correct punctuation mark

❑ makes sense

©2022 Simplify Writing®

2

Review Complete Sentences

The first day, you're focusing on reteaching what a complete sentence is, and how to know it has the required elements. You should model how to use color-coding and/or underlining to label the subject and predicate. If there's time in the same day, you can move straight into some subject and predicate color-coding practice. To continue supporting students with this skill in upcoming lessons, use the same sentence color-coding during your teacher models and student writing time.

Name: _____   Date: _____

Subject and Predicates

Directions: Highlight each part of the sentence using the color key below.

Blue: subject
Yellow: predicate

1. Kathryn eats a snack every day after school.

2. The bicycle chain fell off and broke.

3. Jamie and Amanda went to the library before school.

4. Two dogs chased each other through the backyard.

5. I can't wait to go to Disneyland this summer!

6. The new doctor took a tour of the children's hospital.

7. Our favorite teacher is leaving at the end of the school year.

8. The lady who lives next door grows tomatoes in her garden.

9. Tomorrow I am going to make an appointment at the dentist.

10. Mr. and Mrs. Gellert invited our family over for dinner.

11. My best friend was scared to go in the haunted house alone.

12. Your little brother is so adorable!

©2022 Simplify Writing®

4

Practice Color-Coding Subject and Predicates

This lesson helps prepare students for writing their own sentences by color-coding subjects and predicates. This color-coding only works when students understand each part, instead of simply copying a color-coding pattern. That's why the additional lessons are key in really understanding how to write **and** color-code the complete sentences correctly.

Sentence Sort

Directions: Cut out each group of words below and glue them in the correct place on the chart.

Complete Sentence	Incomplete Sentence

Yesterday, we took Emily hiking at Round Mountain.	Driving though the mountains and watching the birds.
The place that has the highest mountains in the world.	The family brought everything they needed for a picnic.
Bartlett Lake, which is filled with trout for fishing.	Couldn't see anything in the dark, rainy weather.
If you enjoying boating, then you'll love the recreation area.	We gathered all the fishing supplies before taking off.

©2022 Simplify Writing®   5

Identify Complete versus Incomplete Sentences

This lesson allows students to think critically about the rules they learned about complete sentences and apply them. This is important because as they begin to write independently, they will still write incomplete sentences that they will then need to identify as such and correct. I like to do the sentence sorts in partners or groups, and then we review them together and discuss as a class. *The Does It Make Sense?* page is great with partners because it gives the opportunity for them to discuss (or sometimes argue) whether it's a complete subject or not. Discussion and collaborative work is the best way to practice applying the rules at this stage.

Does It Make Sense?

Directions: Read each group of words below and decide whether or not it makes sense as a complete sentence.

	Makes Sense	Doesn't Make Sense
1. I couldn't at the store.		
2. Mr. Charles brought over pizza for dinner.		
3. Octopus eight tentacles.		
4. Your younger sister has.		
5. Last night, Bobby woke up in the middle of the night.		
6. If you want to be on time, you should after.		
7. A dog over there hiding under.		
8. Everyone needs to don't you have it?		
9. The article reported that may people were sick.		
10. I found a website with information the earthquake that happened last year.		

©2022 Simplify Writing®   6

Reflect on Complete versus Incomplete Sentences

Something our writers should constantly be asking themselves is: "Does this make sense?" This is an important part of the writing process, and it's how writers catch mistakes. In this activity, you'll practice asking and answering this key question. This can be used in an interactive way by having students work in groups to compete against each other for the most correct answers. Have students verbally explain their thinking for each one.

Missing Pieces

Directions: Each group of words below is missing a subject or a predicate. Circle the part of the sentence that is missing. Then, rewrite the sentence to make it complete.

1. every afternoon his brother   subject   predicate

_____

2. falling all over the floor   subject   predicate

_____

3. another interesting thing   subject   predicate

_____

4. sticking out from his head   subject   predicate

_____

5. the shiny skin on the jellyfish   subject   predicate

_____

6. an important part of our history   subject   predicate

_____

7

Cross it Off!

Directions: Each paragraph below contains an incomplete sentence. Read each paragraph. Then, cross off the incomplete sentence. Rewrite it correctly below.

1. Have you ever left a chocolate bar in the sun? Gets soft and gooey. However, if you put it in the refrigerator for a few hours, it gets hard again. Then, you can eat it! Heat and cold can change may different materials.

_____
_____
_____

2. Rivers, lakes, and streams hold a tiny amount of the Earth's freshwater. Sometimes, this water can also freeze! For example, many rivers and lakes. Some northern countries like Canada or Norway freeze in the winter.

_____
_____
_____

3. There are many different types of forces besides movements. One interesting force is magnetism. This is an invisible force that can pull on some metal objects. These objects are called magnetic. Some nonmagnetic objects.

_____
_____
_____

4. The different characteristics of animals can help them survive. Sometimes, it's because even animals of the same species might live in different environments. For example, the husky has thick fur. Helps them survive the cold in the Arctic.

_____
_____
_____

8

Correct Mistakes

Many older students who struggle with writing complete sentences simply need to identify incomplete sentences and self-correct. These pages are the best ones for teaching them this skill as it relates to the editing process. These can be used in groups, with partners, or individually, but we always review our answers and discuss as a class. In addition to teaching this as a foundational lesson when my whole class struggles with sentence writing, I often reuse these organizers during the editing process later in the year.

PARAGRAPH WRITING INTERVENTION

There are a lot of different ways students can struggle with writing a paragraph. Even in classes that format their paragraphs correctly, I find they still struggle with organization of the important elements. Essentially, it looks like a paragraph, but is choppy when you read it. This is because indenting the first sentence and grouping sentences is easy to replicate, but actually understanding topic, body, and closing sentences is far more challenging.

When you set the foundation for paragraph writing with these lessons, it allows your students to understand the fundamentals instead of merely replicating how your example looks. When teachers have taught multiple informational units and are still seeing paragraphs that are formatted as paragraphs but missing important elements, I always have them back up to these core lessons. Different writing curriculum uses different color-coding systems, but I've found that yellow (for a slow, careful start), green (go into actual content), and red (stop with a concluding sentence) works best with students.

Topic Sentence	Yellow	Clearly states the main idea of the paragraph
Detail Sentences	Green	Develops the idea with facts, examples, and evidence
Closing Sentence	Red	Restates/summarizes the main idea in a new way

D6.3 Paragraph Writing Lesson

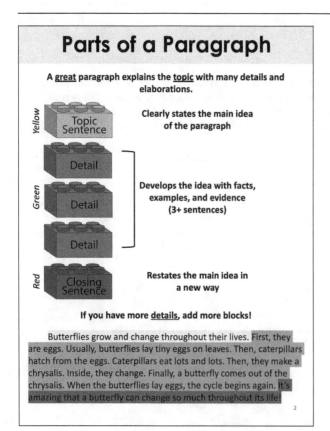

Reteaching the Parts of a Paragraph

In the first lesson, you'll reteach the parts of a paragraph using our color-coding system or the one from your curriculum. Whichever color-coding system you use, make sure to keep it consistent throughout your future lessons. You'll be referring to the parts of a paragraph and the color-coding for every unit where students need to write paragraphs. Many teachers use this note-taking page as the cover page of their student folders or binders because it's *that* important.

Paragraph Structure

Name: _____ Date: _____

Directions: Highlight each part of the paragraph using the color key below.

> **Yellow:** Topic Sentence
> **Green:** Detail Sentences
> **Red/Pink:** Closing Sentence

Think of a person whom you consider to be a hero. Explain why you admire this person.

My grandmother was an amazing person. She worked hard throughout her life, even when she was very old. Every day she cooked, cleaned, and exercised. She was also a good grandmother. Grandma always sent birthday cards and baked cookies for us to eat. Her life taught me how to be a good person.

Explain the similarities and differences between pets and people.

How different are you from your pet dog? Pets and people are similar because we have the same needs. Both pets and people need food, shelter, and water. However, there are many way we're different. People can talk and communicate about complicated things, but animals can't. In conclusion, people and pets are the same in some ways and different in others.

©2021 Simplify Writing®   4

Build a Paragraph

Name: _____ Date: _____

Directions: Cut out each sentence below. Put the strips in order to build a complete paragraph.

Topic Sentence

_____

Details

_____

_____

_____

Closing Sentence

_____

- You'll also need a place that has nutrient-rich soil to feed your plants.
- Most vegetables need 6 to 8 hours of direct sunlight, so be sure to choose a sunny spot.
- Once you've chosen the perfect area, you're ready to start planting your vegetables.
- When planting a vegetable garden, selecting the right location is the key to success.
- Finally, check to make sure the location you choose has proper drainage, so the water doesn't collect in one spot.

©2021 Simplify Writing®   6

Practice Color-Coding

Provide students with ample color-coding practice before having them create their own content to color-code. However, we don't want to stop at this lesson. It's important to continue to learn how to write each part of the paragraph. Otherwise, students will just color-code their paragraph in the same pattern, even if they don't have a topic and closing sentence. There's nothing more frustrating than getting a writing piece that looks like a great paragraph from a distance, but the actual content doesn't match the color-coding.

Build a Paragraph

This activity provides more practice identifying the parts of a paragraph before they have to come up with their own content. This is another great activity to do in partners and groups and then have a class discussion about how we figured out which was the topic sentence, detail sentences, and closing sentence. You can also extend this activity by having students write their own paragraphs, cut into strips, mix, and have their partners put it back together.

Write a Paragraph

Directions: Choose a prompt or think of your own topic. Compose a well-written paragraph that includes a topic sentence, at least three details, and a closing sentence.

Topic Sentence

_____

_____

Details

_____

_____

_____

_____

_____

_____

Closing Sentence

_____

_____

©2021 Simplify Writing®   13

Practice Writing Paragraphs

This page can be used multiple times to help students separate their topic, detail, and closing sentences. Once they use this organizer, have them then copy it down onto a lined paper (or a digital document) so they can format it correctly and highlight. This organizer can also be reused throughout the year if students struggle with body paragraphs during your regular units.

Paragraph Frames

Directions: Fill in the blanks to write your own paragraph.

My favorite book is _____. It was

written by _____. I like this story

because _____.

My favorite part of the book is when _____

_____.

You should definitely read _____!

Learning how to _____

is pretty easy is you follow these simple steps. First, _____

_____.

Next, _____

_____. Then, _____

_____

Finally, _____.

©2021 Simplify Writing®   9

Paragraph Frames

For students who are still working to master sentence writing while you're reteaching paragraphs, using paragraph frames that are already outlined for them can be a huge help. This can also be helpful for students who struggle with starting topic or closing sentences.

Cross it Off!

Directions: Each paragraph below contains a sentence that doesn't belong. Read each paragraph, then cross off the sentence that doesn't fit with the rest of the paragraph.

1. Becoming an astronaut isn't easy. Each year, NASA receives over 12,000 applications during the initial selection period. Once someone is chosen, they must undergo rigorous training in order to prepare for working in outer space. It can take over a year for astronauts to prepare for a mission. In space, astronauts eat freeze-dried food that is stored in disposable packages, but it's actually pretty tasty. Despite the many challenges, being an astronaut is also a very rewarding job.

2. Beverly Cleary is one of the most well-loved children's book authors in America. With over 35 works of fiction, her stories have been published in 29 languages. Cleary's most beloved characters include Ramona Quimby and Henry Huggins. Ramona has an older sister named Beezus. Cleary's books have won several awards, including the 1984 Newbery Award for *Dear Mr. Henshaw*. It's easy to see why Cleary's books will continue to be loved by children for years to come.

3. Did you know that bubble gum has been around for centuries? Early Europeans first began chewing birch bark tar for medicinal purposes. Other plants are also used as medicine, such as the elderberry fruit. In the 1840s, the first commercial gum was created by boiling tree resin and cutting it into strips. However, this spruce gum wasn't very tasty, so manufacturers eventually replaced the ingredients with synthetic material. Bubble gum has definitely changed a lot since it was first invented!

4. When you're learning how to juggle, all you need is a few scarves and a lot of patience! Most experts believe that juggling was first practiced in ancient Egypt. Start by holding one scarf in each hand and tossing them up across your body. Catch each scarf in the opposite hand. Once you've got this motion down, you can try adding a third scarf. Eventually, you can move on to bean bags and then balls. With lots of practice, you'll be a juggling expert in no time!

©2021 Simplify Writing®   8

Revising Paragraphs

In addition to helping students learn the parts of a paragraph, removing sentences that are repetitive or don't belong is an important part of editing their own writing. Give students examples of paragraphs with a sentence or sentences that don't fit for them to cross off. Sentences that do fit with the topic but already repeat something that's been said in the paragraph are also important to identify. In addition to crossing those off, you can also have students create a new sentence that fits with the topic but is unique content.

IDEA GENERATION

Idea generation is an important component of every lesson during the brainstorming and planning phases of our units, but students often struggle to start with the process of coming up with ideas for their graphic organizers. If writing stamina isn't the main issue for your students because they simply can't come up with enough ideas, setting a stronger foundation for idea generation is a good task to begin with.

In the foundational phase, we teach idea generation by teaching students many ways to come up with content. This includes teaching them where ideas for writing come from and strategies to generate fresh ideas to put into their planning organizers. It may seem like common sense to you as an adult, but students often don't have the background knowledge to consider all the different places they can get ideas from.

In addition to students learning the foundations of idea generation, this is a great time for you to put simple procedures into place in your classroom that you will carry into your regular lessons. I have found that teaching students how to properly discuss and research new ideas not only makes their writing more complex, but it allows me to spend less time helping them get started during independent writing time. Because small groups and writing conferences are so important to help fill in gaps for individual students, it's helpful for students to have the tools and knowledge to be self-starters during independent writing time. Being an independent writer is a work in progress with many students, but this lays the foundation for that very important skill.

D6.4 Idea Generation Lesson

Generating Ideas

Where can I get ideas for writing?

Memories & Experiences

Topics I'm Curious About

Places I've Visited

Books & Movies

Things I Care About

The World Around Me

Strategies to Generate Ideas	
❑ Ask questions	❑ Make a list
❑ Discuss with others	❑ Piggyback on another idea
❑ Use a graphic organizer	❑ Research the topic
Remember, some strategies work better for different writing types!	

©2022 Simplify Writing®   2

Teach the Basics

This simple lesson provides a foundation for idea generation. This page is a great way for students to discuss how they can generate complex ideas and what strategies they can use if they get stuck. This is one of the pages that stays in our binders or folders all year for us to refer back to.

Name: _____   Date: _____

Piggybacking

"Piggybacking" is building on another person's idea or using that idea as a starting point to create something new. You can find writing ideas by piggybacking on another story or topic idea.

Original Idea	Piggyback Idea
Writing a story about three little pigs who build different types of houses to protect themselves from a big, bad wolf.	Writing a story about three sisters on a camping trip who create different types of tents that will guard against a storm.
Writing a letter to tell others all about an endangered animal.	Writing a newspaper article to tell others all about a dying plant species.

Directions: Piggyback on each idea below by using the original idea as a starting point to create a new writing piece.

Original Idea	My Piggyback Idea
Writing a newspaper article to convince others to vote for a new law in your community.	
Writing a story about two best friends who have to fight an evil supervillain.	
Explaining how the parts of a donut machine work together to make a donut.	

©2022 Simplify Writing®   4

Learn about Piggybacking

Students often get stuck thinking their ideas need to be totally unique, but we often find inspiration in what other people are doing. This lesson can also start a discussion on what is inspiration versus plagiarism. You can discuss what to do if someone in your group is writing about a topic you like, but you have a special spin to put on it.

Personal Narrative Discussion Questions

Directions: Cut apart the discussion cards below. Mix them up and put them in a stack face down. Turn over a card and read it aloud. Then, take turns answering the question. Take notes about what your group discusses.

Who was there?	When did it happen?
Where did it happen?	How did you feel?
Why does this memory stand out?	How did other people feel?
What do you remember most?	How will it affect you in the future?

©2022 Simplify Writing®   5

Practice Group and Partner Discussion

In the reproducible materials for this chapter, you'll find discussion cards for the different types of writing. I practice using these with students and continue to use them as we get into these units. I recommend you use these along with a journal prompt to learn how to use them. I keep a couple of laminated sets in our writing area in case students get stuck and need to discuss their story with a partner.

Personal Narrative Writing: Make a List

Directions: List 3-4 ideas for each category. Circle the idea you think would make the best writing piece.

Places I've Visited	People I Care About	Special Memories
1. _____	1. _____	1. _____
2. _____	2. _____	2. _____
3. _____	3. _____	3. _____
4. _____	4. _____	4. _____

Skills I Have	My Favorite Things	Important Moments
1. _____	1. _____	1. _____
2. _____	2. _____	2. _____
3. _____	3. _____	3. _____
4. _____	4. _____	4. _____

©2022 Simplify Writing®   9

Practice List-Making

It's never a bad thing to have a list of topics for the different writing types. I usually give my students a specific prompt and a lot of support before beginning each unit, but practicing writing a list of topics is always an important skill.

With all these different idea generation options now in their toolbox, your students will feel much better prepared to tackle coming up with ideas for their writing pieces. I suggest keeping these organizers available for your students who continue to struggle with idea generation throughout the year. The more you can support them with familiar organizers and discussion questions, the more confident they will become in writing!

FINAL THOUGHTS

It may not seem very "simple" to conduct the pre-assessment and tackle these foundational issues, but the work you do during these first two to three weeks will truly simplify your instruction and lesson planning for the rest of the year. With the information you've gathered, you'll find yourself more equipped to handle varying writing abilities. You'll also find that your students have the background knowledge and tools to tackle independent writing activities like paragraph writing and idea generation that they wouldn't have had before.

Most importantly, don't abandon your pre-assessment spreadsheet after Week 3. Make updates to it when your students individually master a concept, or if you notice a student struggling with something that you didn't catch during the pre-assessment. Use the "What this means for my whole group instruction" part of the spreadsheet to modify the lessons in your writing units for your students. Have this spreadsheet open every time you plan a writing lesson throughout the year.

You may also find yourself adding fields or tabs to the spreadsheet, which is encouraged. It feels good to mark off when students master a skill! Your priorities may also shift throughout the year. Your students' need will change throughout the year, and this simple spreadsheet is the best way to keep track of that.

BUILD A FOUNDATION FAQs

HOW DO I FIT IN ALL THESE FOUNDATIONAL ISSUES AND LESSONS INTO ONE TO TWO WEEKS?

No two classes require the same lessons or concepts, so I've included far more lessons than you can fit into this time to allow you to choose what your class needs the most. Instead of trying to fit in everything, prioritize what will make the biggest difference as you head into your regular writing lessons. You don't want to overwhelm your students by cramming in different concepts each day, so be mindful when you choose your lessons for these weeks.

WHAT IF I MUST FOLLOW A RIGOROUS WRITING CALENDAR WITHOUT FLEXIBILITY?

It's common to have a school or district writing calendar, but the autonomy it gives teachers really varies. The truth is, if you have no flexibility with the calendar to account for your class's unique needs, it sets you and your students up to struggle. No one class learns at the same speed, nor do they need the same exact lessons. Respectfully reach out to your principal or instructional coach to share that you need flexibility to differentiate for your students. In many situations, they can advocate for you and your students.

IS THERE A CERTAIN ORDER I SHOULD TEACH FOUNDATIONAL SKILLS?

I usually start with what my whole class struggles with the most in case they need more time on the concept. For example, if my students struggle with paragraph writing and I plan to use the first three days of lessons to reteach it, but they struggle to catch on more than expected, I will use two additional lessons and we won't get to writing stamina. I'll often fit that lesson in somewhere else with one of our future units.

WHAT IF MY STUDENTS DON'T MASTER ONE OF THESE SKILLS? DO I MOVE ON?

You can absolutely move on before your students master these skills. The purpose of the foundational weeks is to introduce them to the concept and give them tools to use in upcoming units. Your students may not have mastered paragraph writing, but you can continue to use your note-taking pages and the color coding to model examples in your on-grade-level lessons throughout the year. I encourage you to continue to use the exact same tools in future lessons to help support your students until they've mastered the concept in their independent writing.

WHAT DO I GRADE WHILE I'M WORKING ON FOUNDATIONAL SKILLS?

I personally only grade our regular units, but I understand that many teachers are required to put a grade in the grade book each week. In this situation, I would give grades for effort instead of mastery. So many of our students are grade levels behind, and it doesn't seem fair to me to grade their writing during foundational practice on grade-level standards. What matters most to me is that they're working hard to meet their goals, no matter what level they're at.

SHOULD I BE TEACHING MY SCHEDULED UNIT WHILE TEACHING THE FOUNDATIONAL LESSONS?

Please do not attempt to teach a regular unit while teaching the foundational lessons. The purpose of these lessons is to help students get extra practice and tools without the pressure of a full writing piece. Although you will continue to build on these lessons during your writing units, it's important to give students the time to really focus on the basics. The one to two weeks you spend on this will not be lost time!

WHAT IF MY STUDENTS IMPROVE THEIR STAMINA, BUT THE WRITING QUALITY IS POOR?

You can't work much with just a few words on paper, but you can work with a lot of unorganized, misspelled words. If your students don't have stamina, independent writing time during your regular units will be a constant struggle. If they improve their stamina, you can work on the quality of the writing in your regular units throughout the year.

SHOULD I START TEACHING GRAMMAR OR SPELLING DURING THE FOUNDATIONAL STAGE?

There's no need to work on grammar or spelling during this stage, as much as it may drive you crazy when you see your class's writing. The "big picture" ideas we're focusing on will help students get writing on their paper in a somewhat organized fashion, then we can tackle the grammatical and spelling issues throughout the year. Chapter 11 discusses how to do that.

WHAT IF THERE ARE A FEW STUDENTS WHO DON'T CATCH ON AFTER A FOUNDATIONAL LESSON?

If you notice that a few students aren't making any progress with these lessons, make a note on the individual section of your pre-assessment section. You will also find yourself updating your spreadsheet for students who just needed a quick reteach and have mastered the concept during the foundational stage.

Reflect and Plan

Get your calendar out and block off 1–2 weeks for teaching the highest priority foundational concepts that your whole class struggles with. Remember not to try to teach every lesson in this chapter. Only use the resources that fit what your entire class needs the most as a group. Reflect on how reteaching these concepts will help set your students up for success for your upcoming on-grade-level lessons.

CHAPTER 7

Use Pre-Assessment Data to Modify Future Lessons

Once you finish your foundational week(s), you and your students will be better prepared to start your on-grade-level lessons. This doesn't mean that you're done with your pre-assessment data or filling in learning gaps. You'll still need to make modifications to your whole group lessons to meet your students where they're at. You'll likely find yourself using some of the same modifications repeatedly throughout the school year. The strategies in this chapter focus on simple, broad changes that you can incorporate into your lesson plans for all your students.

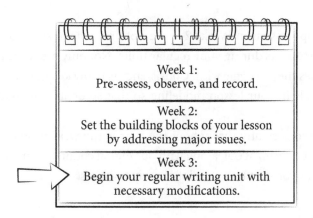

I have more specific strategies for English Language Learners (ELLs) and students with disabilities in Part III of this book, but there are a few general changes you can make during the planning process that work well with a variety of learning abilities. We also haven't discussed yet how to help the students who are struggling with skills that most of your class has mastered. That's more complex, which is why it's not a focus when you're just beginning with this structure. When I share my simple framework for your writing block, I want you to feel prepared to structure your first lessons with these simple modifications.

MODIFY EXPECTATIONS

A simple way to make an on-grade-level assignment work for the varying ability levels of your students is to adjust your expectations. If you have some students below grade level and some above, it's unrealistic to expect them to include the same elements at the same level. For example, in a personal narrative piece, your expectation for the below-grade-level students may be to have a one-page story with two characters and three pieces of dialogue. Your expectations for your above-grade-level students may be a two- to three-page story with multidimensional characters and 10-plus pieces of dialogue. Your on-grade-level students will be expected to fall somewhere in the middle. In this example, you're still teaching about character development and dialogue; you're just modifying what you expect from individual students so that they have a realistic goal for their writing.

FRONTLOAD OR RETEACH

Let's say you're planning for your informational unit, and you notice on your pre-assessment spreadsheet that students struggled with transitions and elaboration. The unit you're using only briefly covers transitions.

Knowing that your students will likely struggle with transitions, you should plan to expand upon the lesson. This information from your pre-assessment allows you to better pace your lessons instead of constantly feeling behind when your students need additional reteach and practice.

If one of the foundational issues you worked on was idea generation, you also can begin your unit by frontloading a lesson on idea generation to set your students up for success. Your regular unit may have a simple graphic organizer to use for brainstorming, but you know from your data and experience that your students are going to need discussion prompts and additional time to outline their content.

USE TOOLS

Your foundational "catch-up" lessons in Weeks 2–3 are not one-time lessons. Use the tools from these lessons to help support your students during your regular units. Not only are these tools familiar to them, but they're targeted for the issues they struggle with. Consistency is really key in writing instruction, so continue to mention and use the tools in your lesson modeling so that students can continue to use them in their own writing.

My favorite tool to use consistently throughout the year is the writing stamina graph. We don't use it every time students write, but I bring it out, along with our digital count-up timer, any time I see my students rushing through their writing or start to have a lot of early finishers.

BANISHING FEELINGS OF BEING OVERWHELMED

You may feel overwhelmed when you first open your pre-assessment spreadsheet to determine how you'll need to modify your lessons. Remember that this spreadsheet represents a year-long plan for filling in gaps for your students. During Quarter 1, you'll focus on simple modification to support your students by looking at the big picture from your pre-assessment. The process of simplifying your writing block, and making it more student-centered, is not going to be put into place the first month.

Reflect and Plan

Reflect on the modification ideas in this chapter. Which do you think will be easiest for you to implement? How will it affect the success of your lessons?

PART THREE

A SIMPLE FRAMEWORK FOR YOUR WRITING INSTRUCTION

Remember to take it slow as you start to implement the strategies in this book. The first quarter is all about data collection and organization and starting your bite-sized lessons. Please practice your regular lessons until you and your students feel comfortable with the format before you attempt to add any of my differentiation strategies, feedback systems, and grammar lessons. You and your students need the time to learn the procedures. Too often, we rush into doing individual writing conferences and small group immediately, and then we struggle because students need too much help during independent writing time.

CHAPTER 8

Prepare Your Classroom

Now that you've laid a strong foundation for your writers, it's time to start your regular writing units with some simple modifications that we discussed in the last chapter. This basic writing block setup will carry you through the school year, and you'll add more advanced elements to it in future months. From a consistent schedule to specific procedures to practice, you'll be well prepared to tackle your first full unit.

WRITING BLOCK SCHEDULE

To have success with writing, your students need a consistent writing block. That means writing should be a priority in your classroom with its own dedicated time at least three times a week. While many teachers have writing blocks as short as 30 minutes, five times a week, others have found better success with a longer block (45–60 minutes) three times a week. Middle school and high school ELA teachers with limited time often block out 2–3 weeks per quarter to focus on just a writing unit.

Your writing block should consist of three simple parts: the whole group mini-lesson, student writing time, and closure. It's important to set a reasonable length of each part so you don't go over every day, causing frustration and taking away from other subject areas. It's also important to respect the 10–15 minute mini-lesson timing so students have ample writing time, but we'll go into that more in the next chapter. Do not split the whole group mini-lesson and student writing time into different days because students need to immediately apply what they learned in their own writing.

WHOLE GROUP MINI-LESSON

This should be between 10 and 15 minutes each day, no more, no less. Less than 10 minutes won't give you enough time to teach the skill you're focusing on, while more than 15 minutes would likely focus on too many skills and overwhelm students. I've found that 10–15 minutes is the perfect length for student attention spans.

INDEPENDENT STUDENT WRITING TIME

During this time, students will apply what they learned during the mini-lesson in their own writing. They may also brainstorm, plan, discuss, and give or receive feedback. It looks different each day, depending on what part of the writing process you're working on. This time is absolutely crucial, so you should have no less than 15 minutes of student writing time during your block. The longer your writing block, the more you can do with this student writing time. This includes peer feedback, conferring with the teacher, revision, and much more.

CLOSURE

If you have a short writing block, your closure time should be brief. You'll quickly remind students what you worked on today, tell them what's coming up tomorrow, and offer praise. If you have a longer writing block, you can include "turn and talk" discussion, share samples, and do even more to celebrate what they worked on that day. This isn't necessary; it's just a nice bonus if you have the additional time.

Sample 3-Part Writing Block Schedules

	Whole Group Mini-Lesson	Student Writing Time	Closure
30 Minute Block	10 min.	15 min.	5 min.
45 Minute Block	15 min.	25 min.	5 min.
60 Minute Block	15 min.	35 min.	10 min.

MEETING PLACE AND STUDENT WORK AREAS

Writing time should be as authentic as possible, so where you do your mini-lessons and student work time matters. Have a meeting place for mini-lessons that has everything you need. This may be in front of a projector, white board, or in a writing area with anchor charts. This meeting space should be rich with books, news articles, supplies, and anything writing-related. If you have room, students can come back and sit in the area with you as you do your whole group lesson. If you have a large class size, and space is limited, students can sit on their desks and face the area. Some teachers have students move desks during writing time to make room for a close-knit area, but extra transition time will need to be built into the writing block for this.

Your student work areas should be fluid with the whole group meeting place. Any writing you create in the meeting place with your class will stay there, and students may wander over to see examples again or get supplies. This is also where I keep my peer feedback forms and any other resources students may need for revision when they "finish" early or get stuck. During independent writing time, open all areas of your classroom for students to use. Some students may prefer to write in groups, while others want a quiet area on a carpet or in the corner. During this time, most students will be writing, but others may be having a discussion or giving feedback using whisper voices. This requires students being able to spread out to different areas for different purposes.

It may seem easier to manage a classroom where students are all seated independently and quietly writing, but it is well worth it to cement procedures in the beginning that allow students to share ideas and resources. In a rigid classroom setup, when students struggle or believe they are finished, the only person they have to help is you as the teacher. This makes it difficult when you start writing conferences or small group because you'll constantly be pulled away from your task. It's much better to spend the first quarter focusing on how they can access resources and have discussions during their independent writing time until they've mastered it.

Photo Credit: Emily Stout

CLASSROOM PROCEDURES

Organization

It's so important to stay organized when you have limited time for a supply-heavy subject like writing. The more organized you and your students are, the easier it will be for them to find the tools and supplies they need to complete their independent writing. I recommend keeping your system simple and consistent for both in-progress work and writing supplies.

My choice for organizing student work is always student writing folders. They're thin enough so that they can all fit into a small storage bin or basket at the end of writing time. I learned the hard way that having students hold onto their in-progress writing pieces is a recipe for disaster. The same goes for having them organize it in a binder that they use for other subjects or take home.

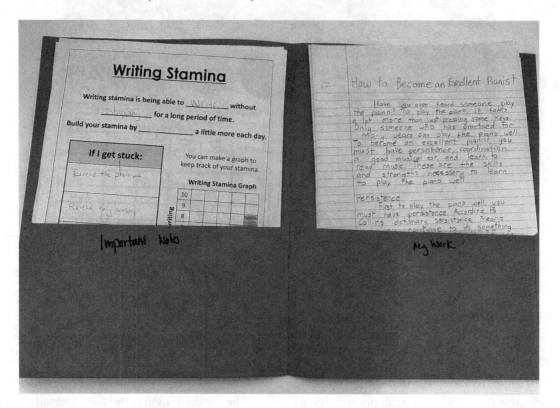

Have your students label the left side of their folder "Important Notes" and the right side "My Work." We keep tools in the left side of the folder, such as the stamina graph, paragraph writing notes, and anything else they may refer to during their independent writing time. On the right side, they keep everything they create in the writing process for the current unit. When students are finished with a writing unit, I staple all of their work together and send it home.

If your students use electronic devices for their independent writing time, you may find that you still need the folders for examples, planning, and other paper. If you're 100% paper-free, your focus should be on modeling how to create and organize digital files for your students. The biggest challenge, other than typing speed and accuracy, is having students find their files. The simplest system is having a folder labeled "Writing" and then a subfolder for each writing unit, such as "Opinion Writing." You will need to consistently model for your students where to save any new files. The fewer files, the better, so I keep all of the students' brainstorming, planning, and other work pages for the unit in one file. They also have a separate document for their writing piece, which makes it easy for them to turn in the final draft when it's time.

Preparing for the Mini-Lesson

The best thing you can do for the transition to your whole group mini-lesson is to keep it simple. Have students bring limited supplies to the meeting place. My preference is to have them just bring themselves and their enthusiasm for writing. I share more about how I simplify our mini-lessons by removing distractions like supplies and note-taking in Chapter 9. No matter how your meeting place is set up, practice how you want students to "get into position." This could be as simple as dismissing them by groups to the meeting place, having them turn and sit on their desks, or moving desks.

If students are leaving their desks to go to the meeting place, you can also have them prepare their supplies for independent writing time during this step. This way, they can go straight from the whole group lesson to their desks with their folder with their work (or computer open to the folder) and all writing supplies needed. If they're staying at their desks, it's important to remove any distractions before beginning the lesson.

Transitioning from Mini-Lesson to Independent Writing Time

With such limited time, it's so important to make this transition efficient. You should model and practice this transition consistently until students have it down. I suggest creating an anchor chart for the transition steps and using a count-up timer to see how long it takes and try to beat your time as your class practices for the first few weeks. You may also find yourself having to rein them back in down the road if this transition is getting sloppy. There are three elements to plan for during this transition:

- Travel time if traveling from one area back to desks.
- Supply preparation.
- Writing folder organization and locating the in-progress writing pieces quickly.

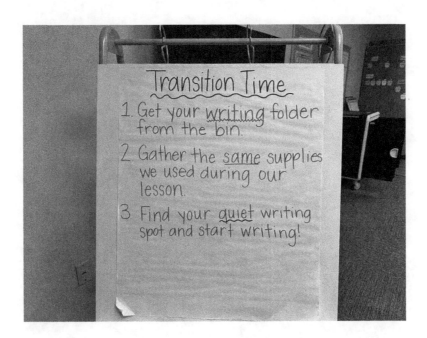

Reflect and Plan

Which simple procedures will you build into your writing block? How will you model these procedures for your students? What will you do when a student struggles with the procedures? Make a solid plan and keep it someplace where you can clearly see it while you and your students practice during your first writing unit.

CHAPTER 9

Start Your First Writing Unit with Efficient Mini-Lessons

One of the struggles we discussed in the beginning of this book is having curriculum that doesn't quite work for your limited writing time and student ability levels. The good news is that any curriculum can be adjusted to fit your needs with a little strategic planning. You can't expect any one curriculum to fit every single classroom, but there are a few things you can do to make it a better fit for you and your students.

If you don't have any curriculum at all, planning a quality mini-lesson can still be a simple process. Curriculum is a helpful way to save time having to create things from scratch, but you can create lessons on the basic steps of the writing process without it. This is what initially led me to create my own lessons that later were refined and became part of the Simplify Writing® program. Keeping in mind the things that *really* matter (see Chapter 2), like quality mini-lessons, is the best way to have success in your writing block.

PLANNING MINI-LESSONS

A writing mini-lesson can be used in various ways in the classroom. It can introduce a new writing skill or concept, such as brainstorming, revising, or using descriptive language, and provide explicit instruction on how to apply it in writing. Teachers can use modeling, think-alouds, and examples to demonstrate the skill or concept, and engage students in discussions and activities to reinforce their understanding. Mini-lessons can also address common writing issues that students may struggle with, such as organization, sentence structure, or punctuation. Teachers can provide strategies, to help students overcome these challenges and enhance their writing proficiency. Additionally, a writing mini-lesson can be used to reteach previously taught writing skills, which we will utilize a lot to fill in learning gaps.

By using writing mini-lessons at the beginning of each writing block, you can scaffold instruction, differentiate learning, and support students in developing their writing skills effectively. This isn't a new or novel idea, but there are specific strategies you need to know in order to make them more efficient and effective. This chapter is all about overcoming the past struggles you've had with writing mini-lessons and making your new lessons more targeted and differentiated for your students.

THE IMPORTANCE OF "BITE-SIZED" MINI-LESSONS

Most teachers are familiar with mini-lessons, short 10- to 15-minute whole group lessons, but they also struggle to not go over this time limit. The most common story I hear is that student writing time is always short or nonexistent because the whole group lesson goes over its time allotment. This is usually because we're trying to squeeze as much learning as possible into every lesson. More often than not, our curriculum is pushing us to do the same, or it's meant for a classroom that has a much longer writing block.

When you give a whole group mini-lesson in writing, it's important to focus on one small, bite-sized skill that students can easily replicate during their own writing time. A full writing unit may take three to four weeks to complete, depending on your schedule. This may seem like slow pacing at first, but breaking it down gives us the chance to take a deep dive into each skill and really improve upon student writing proficiencies.

When I started breaking my writing mini-lessons into smaller chunks in my own classroom, I noticed a few things:

- Student retention increased.
- Student focus improved.
- Students had more time to apply the skill in their own writing.
- I felt less rushed.
- Students needed less help during independent writing time.

	Focused "Bite-Sized" Skill	Overwhelming Mini-Lesson
Learning Goal	Students illustrate and write down the most important events for the beginning, middle, and end of their story.	Students discuss, brainstorm, and plan their personal narrative.
Whole Group Lesson	The teacher models using one simple organizer to sketch the parts of their own story.	The teacher shows multiple steps and organizers, possibly going over the mini-lesson time.
Independent Writing Time	The students use the same organizer to sketch the parts of their story.	The students only complete part of the process because there are too many steps and organizers to remember.

One of my favorite mini-lessons in my personal narrative unit is called "Sketch It Out", which will be used as an example in this chapter. It's just one small piece of our planning process, which we focus on for several days in order to get high-quality ideas before students start their rough drafts. Narrative is especially difficult for students to master because they often leave out important events, character dialogue, setting development, and other elements that make the story interesting. So, planning for each of those pieces on separate days helps students easily incorporate the multiple features of narrative writing.

While you're planning your daily lessons, make sure to ask yourself: "Can students easily do this step in the time we have for independent writing time?" If the answer is no, break the lesson into two parts. Not only will this help prevent students who are behind in the writing process, but it will cause less stress on you and your students overall.

BIRD'S-EYE VIEW PLANNING

Whether or not you have a set writing curriculum, the first step for planning your mini-lessons is to write out each step of the writing process. Break the full unit into small chunks where students learn one skill each lesson. Use notes and observations from your pre-assessment data to pinpoint areas where your whole class may struggle and add or extend lessons on that concept in your plan. This may mean that a single, overwhelming lesson on body paragraphs in your current curriculum turns into a three-day lesson with skills like transition/topic sentences, evidence and analysis, and wrap-up sentences broken into their own lessons.

Next, calendar these days out over a month. If you end up having any additional days after holidays and events, add a "catch-up" day in areas where you think students may fall behind. A place where I often need to pause is after the body paragraph mini-lessons are complete. Even though I break the body paragraph down into small chunks for my mini-lesson and give them ample time to work on those skills in their own pieces, this is the part I find students struggle to complete the most. An extra day for some to catch up, while others get to improve upon their body paragraphs, is always a win for me.

Example Unit Pacing 4th-Grade Personal Narrative	
Day 1	Elements of Personal Narrative
Day 2	Brainstorming Ideas
Day 3	Planning: Sketch Notes
Day 4	Planning: Setting Description
Day 5	Draft: Introduction
Day 6	Draft: Beginning Elements
Day 7	Draft: Middle Elements
Day 8	Draft: Focus on Dialogue
Day 9	Draft: Ending Elements
Day 10	Draft: Conclusion
Day 11	Revision
Day 12	Editing
Day 13	Introduction to Publishing
Day 14	Publishing & Final Proofread
Day 15	Publishing

DAILY PLANNING

The most important thing to remember about your daily lesson planning is that it needs to be sustainable. Complicated lessons and lesson plans make it difficult to focus on what really matters in writing instruction. For this reason, I give teachers a one-page lesson plan template with the instruction to use what's needed and skip the rest. For some teachers, having every element of the planning page filled out helps them better focus their lesson. For others, the bulleted process is all they need. Use only what you need on this lesson plan template to guide your instruction.

In a perfect world, you would plan all your daily lessons together as a unit. This means sitting down for two to three hours to outline the lessons and create your teacher models for the unit. With our limited and sometimes sporadic planning time, it's often only possible to plan one week at a time. No matter how you plan your daily lessons, remember to keep each one simple. If you're spending several hours a week creating lessons plans and teacher models, the lessons are too complex.

You also need to leave some wiggle room in your plans to make changes. You may sometimes find that your class struggles with a skill even after your mini-lesson. This is a sign to break down the skill further and reteach before moving on. Don't let the stress of "getting it done" get in the way of helping your students master this skill. Remember, it's nearly impossible for a curriculum, or even the lessons you created for your students, to always have the perfect pacing for your group.

Your daily lesson plan will be built around a simple teacher model that teaches students the skill and shows them how to put it into place in actual writing. For example, on Day 3 of our Personal Narrative unit, we sketch out and briefly describe the basic story events from beginning to end. The teacher model introduces the graphic organizer and shows the process in the same exact way that students will do it on their writing pieces. You'll notice on the lesson plan that the mini-lesson steps the teacher takes are similar to the student's steps during independent writing time.

UNIT: PERSONAL NARRATIVE WRITING – DAY 3 EXAMPLE LESSON PLAN

Purpose: I can begin to develop a story that has a beginning, middle, and end by planning the most important events in my narrative.

Standard(s):
- CCSS.ELA-LITERACY.W.4.3: Write narratives to develop real or imagined experiences or events using effective technique, descriptive details, and clear event sequences.
- CCSS.ELA-LITERACY.W.4.3.A: Orient the reader by establishing a situation and introducing a narrator and/or characters; organize an event sequence that unfolds naturally.

Materials
Print
- Teacher model
- Student organizer

Learning Goal

Students will illustrate and write down the most important events for the beginning, middle, and end of their story.

Success Criteria

- **Criterion 1** - The student generates an event sequence with events in the beginning, middle, and end of the story organizer.
- **Criterion 2** - The events are in the order they happened.

Mini-Lesson Steps (10–15 min.):

1. Review the narrative prompt from Day 2. Have students refer back to their "Brainstorming" graphic organizer to remember the topic they chose to write about. Tell students that it is important to plan the sequence of narrative events so that they have an outline before they begin to write.
2. Display "Planning: Sketch It Out," explaining each part to students. Using your teacher model, *Helping Others at the Food Bank*, show how an author can sketch out the beginning, middle, and end and add quick notes to remember details, stay organized, and keep events in sequential order. Allow students to provide input as you complete it together.

Student Portion (15–30 min.):

1. Distribute "Planning: Sketch It Out" for students to begin brainstorming the major events of their selected topic.
2. Students will sketch illustrations to show their personal narrative's beginning, middle, and end.
3. Students should add brief notes to their drawings to sequence events.
4. Provide individual conferring to students as needed.

Closure (5–7 min.):

1. Students will pair and share their planning page. Partners will give constructive feedback as necessary.

Parts of Your Lesson Plan

Purpose	Write a simple "I can" statement that tells what one skill the lesson focuses on. Always start with the purpose to help guide you in planning the day's lesson.
Standard(s)	Include any standards this lesson meets if you need to keep a record. You can also check off the standards for the unit during the "bird's-eye view planning" and skip this step on individual lessons.
Materials	What materials will you and your students need for this lesson? Don't overcomplicate this. A teacher example and basic writing tools should be sufficient unless something needs to be color-coded. With color-coding, I use colored pencils because they're cheaper than highlighters.
Learning Goal	Take your purpose and turn it into a goal that represents what students should be able to do independently in their own writing.
Success Criteria	Write what success looks like during independent writing time. This should be the same as what you modeled in your writing piece.
Mini-Lesson Steps & Model	Briefly outline the steps you will show in your mini-lesson and teacher model.
Student Portion	Your students should complete the same steps you did in your model, so this should be similar to the mini-lesson steps.
Closure	Wrap up your lesson. If you have less than 5 minutes for this, give your whole class positive feedback and tell them what you're working on tomorrow. In many classrooms, there isn't much time for closure. If you have a longer writing block, you can incorporate activities that involve sharing their work.

Unit: _____

Date: _____

Purpose: I can **Standard(s):**

Materials
-
-
-
-

Learning Goal

Success Criteria

Mini-Lesson Steps (10-15 min.):

Student Portion (15-30 min.):

Closure (5-7 min.):

File D9.1 Blank Lesson Template File

THE SECRET SAUCE: A WELL-PLANNED TEACHER MODEL

If you take away one thing from this chapter, I want it to be the importance of having a teacher model for each of your daily lessons. A concrete example is the best way for students to learn the skill and understand your expectations during their writing time. Pre-planning your model allows you to incorporate the skills you want your students to use in their own writing. When you come up with examples on the fly, you miss important elements, or your lesson goes over your time because you're having to stop to think it through.

In Kelly Boswell's book, *Every Kid a Writer*, she compares a mentor text to a picture on the box of a jigsaw puzzle. She says, "Modeling, or teacher demonstration, goes a step beyond." We introduce students to high-quality writing in mentor texts, but we still need to show the process an author takes to turn the ideas in their head into a well-polished text (Boswell, 2020).

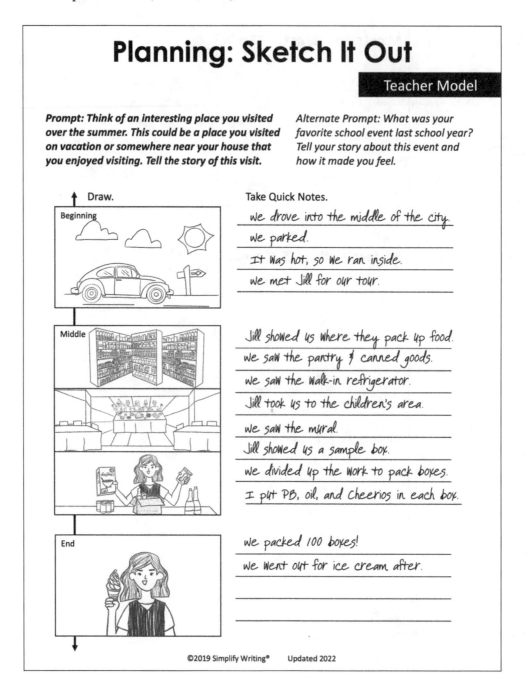

Planning: Sketch It Out

Teacher Model

Prompt: Think of an interesting place you visited over the summer. This could be a place you visited on vacation or somewhere near your house that you enjoyed visiting. Tell the story of this visit.

Alternate Prompt: What was your favorite school event last school year? Tell your story about this event and how it made you feel.

Draw.

Take Quick Notes.

Beginning

we drove into the middle of the city.

we parked.

It was hot, so we ran inside.

we met Jill for our tour.

Middle

Jill showed us where they pack up food.

we saw the pantry & canned goods.

we saw the walk-in refrigerator.

Jill took us to the children's area.

we saw the mural.

Jill showed us a sample box.

we divided up the work to pack boxes.

I put PB, oil, and Cheerios in each box.

End

we packed 100 boxes!

we went out for ice cream after.

©2019 Simplify Writing®   Updated 2022

It's important to create a teacher model that is very simple. Not only will you complete this model in front of your students during a 10- to 15-minute mini-lesson, but your students will also be expected to do the same amount of work during their writing time. Anything too complex will cause you to go over your lesson time and be left with many students who are behind on their own writing pieces. In the "Sketch It Out" example, I only draw five main events for the beginning, middle, and end of the story. I then break down those events a bit by writing key points next to each image. These are short and sweet because we'll learn how to expand upon them in our upcoming lessons.

This pre-planned model makes your whole group mini-lesson incredibly simple. When it's time to teach the lesson, have your completed model next to you for reference. Give your students a brief overview of what you'll be learning in this lesson, then use the model to actively write with your students. Some teachers like to use anchor chart paper for this. Others project their work, either on paper or as a digital file. No matter how you prefer to display your model, make sure you're doing the entire process *with* your students. You should start each lesson how your students will start (whether with a graphic organizer, blank lined paper, or in-progress rough draft) and end how your students will end. Use your pre-planned model as a guide to use during your lesson, but be open to making changes based on student responses or suggestions. Each lesson will build off of the last, so your students should see your writing piece come together as theirs does as well.

Another benefit of using a teacher model for your mini-lessons is that you can naturally model grammar or organizational skills by making mistakes and correcting them in front of the class. You don't want to go into a full grammar lesson in the middle of your model, but you can make a few purposeful mistakes while you're writing and have students help you correct them. Try to keep these mistakes short and quick to assess, so you don't take away from your main lesson or go over time.

IMPLEMENTING MINI-LESSONS

Implementing your well-planned writing mini-lessons is simple with the right systems in place. However, even the best laid plans can go astray. Your implementation will not always go smoothly, especially in the beginning. There are some common pitfalls you can avoid, which we discuss in this chapter.

Keeping Students Engaged

Using an interesting model is a simple way to get students engaged in your mini-lesson. Nevertheless, there are many ways that you can lose engagement or struggle with management during your model. The great news is that you don't need anything fancy to get your students engaged in your lessons.

What *not* to do	What *to* do
Call on individual students during the lesson.	Have students write down any burning questions they have, then answer them at the beginning of independent writing time.
Have students take detailed notes.	Leave your teacher model and any notes you take displayed for students to use. You can do this with anchor charts, a binder of your models for the entire unit, or a digital folder.
Have just one student share.	Include questions where students can all respond at the same time by shouting out an answer or showing on their hands (thumbs up/thumbs down, show me 1, 2, or 3, etc.).
Write for a long period of time.	Break up your model writing by asking students questions or for feedback.

The easiest way to lose engagement is by making your students feel like they're not involved in the task. This can happen when you call on individual students to ask questions or share, or if you turn your back to them to write without speaking to them. The best way to keep a high engagement during your mini-lesson is to make students feel like they're needed. Continuously talk to your entire group of students throughout your writing model. I constantly prompt my students for comments and thank them for their help and feedback while I'm working on my writing piece.

It may be an unpopular opinion, but note-taking during the mini-lesson is a huge distraction and takes too much time. The students who struggle with note-taking are often the ones who need to stay focused on the lesson the most to understand it. Students retain more by being actively involved in the process than they do by taking notes, so I prioritize active engagement over note-taking during my mini-lessons.

So, how do you actively engage your class for 10–15 minutes? It's all about immersing them in the lesson by prompting them to share ideas or help with your writing piece as a group. It may be helpful to come up with some ideas of questions you'll ask them to keep them involved. Some simple ideas for our *Sketch It Out* lesson follow.

Active Engagement Ideas for the *Sketch It Out* Mini-Lesson

1. "Think about the writing prompt we started yesterday: we are writing about an interesting _____ " (students should respond chorally to fill in the blank: <u>place</u>).
2. "Turn to a partner and, in one sentence, tell them about the place you chose to write about."
3. "Give me a thumbs-up once you have your copy of the mentor text on your desk and are ready to reread."
4. "We only want to draw the main events that are important to telling the story about the visit to the food bank. I'm going to say a plot event that the author could have chosen to draw on the sketch notes. Give me a thumbs-up if it is important to the story and a thumbs-down if it's not necessary to include." (List plot events from the teacher model example and include other events – see the following examples that are not important to include.)
   1. I woke up and brushed my teeth.
   2. I was wearing a pink T-shirt.
   3. I stopped working to tie my shoe.
   4. I washed my hands and threw the paper towel in the trash can.
5. "Look at this sketch I drew. I want to write a brief note to help me remember the sequence. Help me fill in each note: First, we _____ (students respond chorally "drove to the food bank"). Next, we _____. Then, we _____."
6. "Show me with your fingers on a scale of 1–5 how you feel about getting started on your own sketch notes. Show me a 5 if you understand the directions completely and are ready to go. Show me a 3 if you are feeling okay about it but maybe have a question you need me to answer. Show me a 1 if you are completely confused and need more help before you get started."

You'll find that your students remember more of your lesson when you use this active engagement technique. You'll see an increase in confidence since they helped you do in your writing model what they'll do in their pieces. They will also prompt themselves with similar questions when they work on this task in their own writing.

INDEPENDENT WRITING TIME

Independent writing time is best described as a time of self-directed learning where students can work on their writing skills at their own pace with the guidance and support of the teacher. It allows students to take ownership of their learning and to develop their writing skills in a safe and supportive environment. However, there's so much more that happens during this time that's not fully independent work.

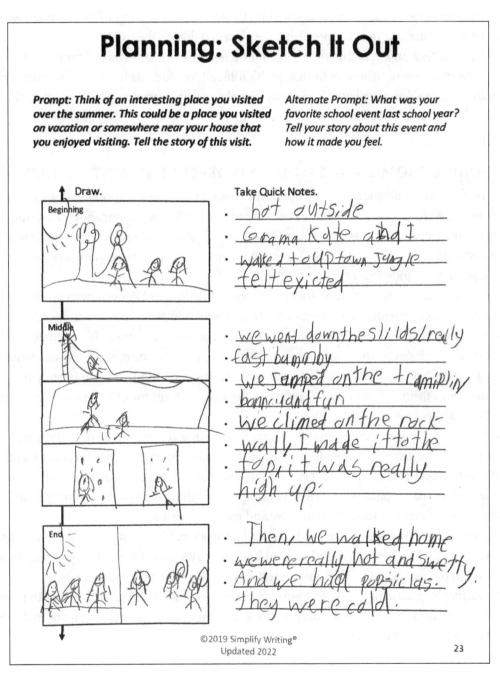

Sketch Notes Student Sample

Once you and your students have mastered the writing block procedures, you can use this block of time directly after the mini-lesson for additional strategies that support individual needs and fill in gaps. These strategies include:

- Small Group (Chapter 12)
- Writing Conferences (Chapter 13)
- Peer Feedback (Chapter 14)

Start with the basics for your independent writing time before adding any of these strategies. It's key for students to be able to use this time to apply what they learned during the mini-lesson in their own writing. They should have at least an equal amount of time for their own writing as you did for your model, and this time needs to be in the **same session** as the lesson. It's difficult for students to remember what to do in their writing if they do it on a different day as the lesson, so make sure they are doing the same thing in their writing immediately after you model it.

TRANSITIONING FROM MINI-LESSON TO INDEPENDENT WRITING TIME

The transition from your mini-lesson to independent writing time can be smooth and seamless with clear procedures and a lot of practice. First, ensure that you provide explicit directions about what students should do next during the closure portion of your mini-lesson. Teach students how to refer to your teacher model during their writing time if they get stuck. The more unambiguous you make your directions, the quicker students can get to work independently.

Make sure your students have the tools they need for writing time and know how to use them before they leave your mini-lesson. Provide the students who need it with additional tools to use, such as a checklist, stamina graph, word bank, bilingual glossary (ELLs), rubric, or sentence frames. It's acceptable to send most of your students to their desks, while keeping a small group to provide one of these tools and instruction on how to use it. Once they become familiar with these tools, they can use them consistently or access them only when they need them. You'll find more information on these tools for ELLs and students with learning disabilities in Chapters 15 and 16.

Have a clear set of procedures for this transition and for the remainder of your independent writing block. Your procedures may vary depending on what students are doing during this time. It's important to practice the basic procedures consistently before adding anything more complex to the writing block. Until most of your students have mastered what to do during writing time, you shouldn't start meeting with small groups or allowing students to independently give and receive peer feedback.

Take the time to review expectations for behavior and work habits as often as you need. This will help students understand what is expected of them and how to work more effectively during the session. Some groups may catch on quickly. For others, they may be practicing these procedures for weeks or months. Let students know they're practicing this so that you can eventually work more individually with them through conferences and small groups. There is a purpose for each procedure, and each one helps make the writing block a more productive experience for them.

Procedures to Practice

Procedure	What It Looks Like
Assigning the Task	During your mini-lesson closure, provide clear and concise instructions on what students should do during the session, and what materials or resources they will need. When used in conjunction with your teacher model, these instructions will help students understand what to do and to stay on task. This is a good time to provide an opportunity for students to ask questions and to clarify any confusion before the independent writing session begins.
Preparing to Write	Model for students which resources and supplies to get ready to prepare for their own writing. Have students practice by displaying a "count-up" timer to see how long it takes them. Make this a competition as you practice this procedure. There's no need to time them once they've mastered it, but you can use the timer method again if the process slows down in the future.
Optional: Mastering Flexible Seating Rules	We discussed using flexible seating to make writing time special and accommodate students who need to work in a quieter area. Instruct students on how to choose their seating during independent writing time and help them learn which environment best suits their needs. This is also a good time to share the rules for flexible seating and what will happen if they are not following these directions. Set these guidelines early on and be consistent with enforcing them if you are using flexible seating.
Starting Independent Writing	Use a signal, such as a bell or a chime, to indicate when the student writing session is about to begin and when it is over. This helps students transition smoothly by prompting them to begin and end the same way each day.
Setting the Tone	Model a quiet and focused environment during the writing session to minimize distractions and to help students concentrate on their writing. Once students have mastered this, more autonomy can be given by allowing them to work with partners for activities like peer-to-peer feedback.
Getting Support and Feedback	This is the trickiest procedure because without a good system in place, teachers have no way to step away for small groups or conferences without having to constantly manage certain students. Set a system to periodically check in with students to ensure they are on task and to provide support, guidance, and feedback. When you're unavailable to provide them with help, have a procedure in place for what they should do if they're stuck or finished early. Make sure there is a cue they recognize for when you are unavailable—such as an accessory you wear, a sign you put out, etc.

REINFORCING SKILLS DURING INDEPENDENT WRITING TIME

The good news is that everything you're teaching during your mini-lesson is helping reinforce these skills in student writing. Not only are you modeling good writing by providing examples and discussing the elements of strong writing, but you're also showing students what it looks and sounds like for each step of the writing process. Students can translate this directly into their writing piece, and they retain the information through practicing that skill.

Six Ways to Reinforce Writing Skills during Independent Writing Time

1. Provide clear guidelines and expectations for each step of the writing process.
2. Model writing by providing examples and discussing the elements of robust writing.
3. Encourage students to revise and edit their own work, using a writing rubric or checklist as a guide.
4. Offer additional writing opportunities, such as journaling or writing contests, to give students more practice and the chance to showcase their skills.

5. Provide time for peer review and feedback, which can help students learn from their fellow students and improve their writing through constructive criticism.

6. Offer extra help or support for students who may need it, such as one-on-one writing conferences or small group workshops.

There are definite challenges that come with independent writing time, but it's manageable with a simple plan in place. The most common issue teachers have during this time is students who are stuck or finish early. Chapter 10 focuses on tools to use for these students, so you can manage these issues and still have time to do small group and confer.

MINI-LESSON FAQs

SHOULD I FILL OUT MY TEACHER MODEL BEFORE THE LESSON?

Absolutely not! The most you should do is outline the graphic organizer or prepare a blank organizer. Your students will learn best if they see your entire writing process, then apply these skills in their writing process directly after.

WHAT SHOULD I DO IF ONE OF MY MINI-LESSONS GOES OVER TIME?

First, give yourself some grace. This happens to the best of us. If your lesson goes over time, it will directly affect the time your students have to write independently. If the time left for student writing is so short that most of them will fall behind, allow them to start their writing, but push back tomorrow's lesson to help catch up. The next day, give a five-minute reminder lesson using the teacher model and give students the time they need to finish their own writing. Pushing back your lessons a day occasionally isn't a big deal, but this can cause a pacing issue over time if it happens too often. If you find this is happening a lot, break your lessons into smaller chunks, or check the "what not to do" in the preceding table to see if one of these items is causing your lessons to go too long.

WHAT IF MY STUDENTS COPY MY TEACHER MODEL WORD FOR WORD?

The biggest concern teachers have when modeling their own writing directly before having students do the same task in their writing is that students will copy their model instead of using their own thoughts. This is rare in most classes, but there are a few things you can do to prevent it. First, add more discussion to your student writing time. This will naturally help students expand upon their ideas. If that's not enough, use our idea generation lessons and organizers to help students come up with their own content. If you have struggling students copying your model word for word, it's not necessarily a bad thing. They're learning formatting and sentence structure as they copy. Small group or writing conference time is a great time to help them add to their copied text or make small tweaks to make it their own. Learning looks different for all students, so we should use any opportunity we can get to help them improve their skills.

SHOULD GRAMMAR BE PART OF MY MINI-LESSON?

Grammar will naturally be a part of everything you do during your writing block, whether it's on the lesson plan or not. There are a lot of great ways to include grammar in your mini-lessons. Most teachers balance grammar by using it intuitively in the mini-lesson while also sometimes giving small group or whole group lessons dedicated to a specific grammar skill that students are struggling with. Head to Chapter 11 to learn more about your options for incorporating grammar.

WHAT IF MY STUDENTS STILL CAN'T GET STARTED ON THEIR INDEPENDENT WRITING AFTER MY MINI-LESSON?

If your mini-lesson models the exact skill that students will be doing in their writing, most of your students will intuitively be able to move into independent writing time without delay. However, for the students who can't start, a checklist can be a very helpful tool. If you find that many of your students are struggling to get started writing, use the end of your mini-lesson time to have students help you recap the steps you took in your writing to make a checklist that they can follow in their own writing. If they're still struggling, you may have to use an idea generation technique like partner discussion to get them going.

HOW DO I HELP STUDENTS WHO ARE BELOW GRADE LEVEL?

Once your writing block is in place and everyone is comfortable with the expectations and procedures, you'll be able to start working with students in small groups on the below-grade-level skills they need to master. If you haven't started small groups yet, or you have students below grade level who aren't currently in your small group for the day, modifying expectations is the best way to support them. They'll be writing to the same prompt, but their modified goal may be to only write one paragraph instead of a full piece. There are more examples for this situation in the differentiation and small group pages of this book.

WHAT IF I TEACH TWO GRADE LEVELS AT THE SAME TIME? DO I TEACH THE SAME LESSON?

The good news is that the writing standards are a progression from one year to the next, so they have the same core elements. Teaching two lessons would likely take valuable time that you could be spending in small group with students. The simplest way to handle this is to teach one lesson for all students, focusing on natural differentiation opportunities within that lesson. Most classrooms have writers at a lot of different ability levels, so this won't be any different. If you need to build on a skill to hit a specific standard, you can always start at the lower grade level standard and dismiss those students while you add one more step for the higher grade level students, but it's unlikely you'll need to do this.

Reflect and Plan

What will your planning process look like for writing? What will you prioritize in your lesson plans? Plan your first unit starting with the bird's-eye view, and then sectioning it into "bite-sized" lessons so that your students can master the skills they need for their writing process.

CHAPTER 10

Prepare for Early Finishers and Students Who Are Stuck

Early finishers and students who need help are the most difficult management issues to overcome during independent writing time. This is why I don't start doing small group or individual writing conferences until we've had several weeks to practice procedures. The most popular tools I use during this time are hint bookmarks, elaboration cards, and peer feedback forms. Take the time to teach your students how to independently use these tools and be consistent about it throughout the year. Teaching students to be self-sufficient during writing time is a big job at first, but it pays off in improved writing pieces and teacher time saved over the year.

There are also a lot of great organizers you can reuse from the foundational lessons you taught the first few weeks. My students often reuse their writing stamina and idea generation pages to push themselves further during independent writing time. In addition, having a procedure for peer feedback is very helpful for early finishers or students who are stuck. My peer feedback lesson and more specific procedures are in Chapter 14 if you want to incorporate that into your writing block.

I also provide one or two resources with each unit for students who are stuck or finished early. These are specific to the unit and are usually discussion questions or checklists that go with the writing type. We review these resources and how to use them at the start of our unit, and I direct students to them as needed during independent writing time. Once your class has used these tools for a few units, students will feel more confident using them independently and most will automatically make it over to your writing area to pick a copy up when they need one. The same can be said for our peer feedback forms.

As with most of the resources in this book, these are meant to be used one or two at a time, after modeling them for students and helping them practice how to use them. You may use all of these resources over the course of a year, or only a handful. Use only what your students need and what best fits your writing unit at the time. It's a lot easier if you reuse the same activities because consistency makes everything simpler.

Feeling Stuck?

1. Think: Where are you stuck?
   - ❑ Beginning/Introduction Paragraph
   - ❑ Middle/Body Paragraphs
   - ❑ End/Conclusion Paragraph
   - ❑ Other: _____
2. Review the teacher model.
3. Get peer support.
4. Ask yourself: What other tools are available to me?
   - ❑ Reflection questions
   - ❑ Research the topic
   - ❑ Piggyback on another idea
   - ❑ Other: _____

©2022 Simplify Writing®   2

Feeling Stuck? Anchor Chart
This general checklist can be made into an anchor chart to hang in your writing area, or you can keep copies for students to grab if they're stuck. This encourages students to identify where they're stuck, review the teacher model, and then use resources if they're still stuck. Peer support is a big element of the writing process in a dynamic writing classroom, but it's something you need guidelines and procedures in place for. This doesn't mean that students should just go find a friend any time they need help. See Chapter 14 for the peer feedback structure.

Feeling Stuck?

1. Think: Where are you stuck?
   - ❑ Beginning/Introduction
   - ❑ Middle/Body Paragraphs
   - ❑ End/Conclusion
   - ❑ Other: _____
2. Review the teacher model.
3. Get peer support.
4. Ask yourself: What other tools are available to me?
   - ❑ Discussion questions
   - ❑ Research the topic
   - ❑ Piggyback on another idea
   - ❑ Other: _____

©2022 Simplify Writing®

Feeling Stuck?

1. Think: Where are you stuck?
   - ❑ Beginning/Introduction
   - ❑ Middle/Body Paragraphs
   - ❑ End/Conclusion
   - ❑ Other: _____
2. Review the teacher model.
3. Get peer support.
4. Ask yourself: What other tools are available to me?
   - ❑ Discussion questions
   - ❑ Research the topic
   - ❑ Piggyback on another idea
   - ❑ Other: _____

©2022 Simplify Writing®   3

Feeling Stuck? Bookmarks
If your students get stuck often, you can print these bookmarks on colored paper and laminate them for use throughout the year. There's also a version of the bookmark titled "Finished Early?" that you can print on the back and have one bookmark for both occasions. Have students keep their bookmark in their writing folder for when they need it.

Teacher Model Review

Directions: Use the teacher model or a mentor text to answer the questions below.

My Topic: _____

What portion of the teacher model should I review?	
What does the teacher model do well?	
How can I use this example in my own writing?	

©2022 Simplify Writing®   4

Teacher Model Review

One of the procedures listed on the checklist for students who are stuck is to review the teacher model. Often students will walk back to it (or pull it up on their screen if it's digital) and they'll remember something from the lesson that they need to do in their writing. Sometimes, they will review the teacher model and still be stuck. This organizer helps support students in this situation. You can post these questions next to your model, or you can leave copies of this organizer for students to fill in.

Peer Support

Directions: Complete the top portion of this form. Then, find a peer to ask for support. Share your writing so far and complete the bottom portion of this form with your partner.

My Topic:

I am feeling stuck with	Questions I have

Questions my peer has about my writing	Suggestions	What I did with these suggestions

©2022 Simplify Writing®   5

Peer Support

For those of you not interested in incorporating a full peer feedback system, this is a good way to dip your toes into students getting feedback from each other. If a student is stuck, they'll fill in the top part of the organizer. Then, they'll work with their partner or someone else in the class to get help, which they will write on the bottom part. See Chapter 14 on peer feedback for expanded information on how to choose where students can go for help instead of interrupting other students who are actively working on their own pieces.

Informational/Explanatory
Reflection Question Cards

Informational/Explanatory	Informational/Explanatory
What do I already know about the topic?	**What resources could I use to learn more about the topic?**
Informational/Explanatory	Informational/Explanatory
What people are associated with the topic?	**What dates or time periods are associated with the topic?**
Informational/Explanatory	Informational/Explanatory
What specific places are associated with the topic?	**How does this topic affect me? How does it affect others?**
Informational/Explanatory	Informational/Explanatory
Why is this topic important?	**What aspects of the topic am I most curious about?**

©2022 Simplify Writing®   9

Informational/Explanatory Reflection Question Cards

These reflection question cards are specific to the type of writing, and they're a great way for students to ask themselves questions about their writing. These questions often spark thinking that leads to them adding great details to their writing piece. These very basic question cards can be laminated and put in the writing area for students to use as they need them. I like to keep 5–10 sets so that every student who needs one can have a set. I bundle each set together with a rubber band.

Research Form

Directions: Use the organizer to gather more information about your topic.

My Topic:

Questions I Still Have	Resources I Can Use to Learn More	What I Learned

Where will I use this information in my writing?

©2022 Simplify Writing®   11

Research Form

Often when students get stuck, they lack either inspiration or information. If your unit involves research, and students have books or websites they can use to further research their topic, this organizer can be used to help them get more information for their writing. This can help them generate ideas that go straight into their writing pieces. When we're creating information pieces, I like to check out a lot of books from the library on the topic(s) for students to get information from. This graphic organizer is a great companion to any informational book used for research. Students especially love doing research using informational picture books!

Piggybacking

Feeling Stuck?

"Piggybacking" is building on another person's idea or using that idea as a starting point to create something new. You can find writing ideas by piggybacking on another story or topic idea.

Original Idea	Piggyback Idea
Writing a story about three little pigs who build different types of houses to protect themselves from a big, bad wolf.	Writing a story about three sisters on a camping trip who create different types of tents that will guard against a storm.
Writing a letter to tell others all about an endangered animal.	Writing a newspaper article to tell others all about a dying plant species.

Directions: Piggyback on each idea below by using the original idea as a starting point to create a new writing piece.

Original Idea	My Piggyback Idea
Writing a newspaper article to convince others to vote for a new law in your community.	
Writing a story about two best friends who have to fight an evil supervillain.	
Explaining how the parts of a donut machine work together to make a donut.	

©2022 Simplify Writing®   12

Finished Early?

1. Reread your writing.

2. Use a sentence starter to add more details.

3. Elaborate on your ideas.
   - ❏ What does it mean?
   - ❏ Why is it important?
   - ❏ How does it connect to your main idea?

4. Ask for feedback by completing the Feedback Form.
   - ❏ Peer
   - ❏ Teacher
   - ❏ Family Member

5. Use the Revision Checklist to revise your writing.
   - ❏ Add or remove details
   - ❏ Reorganize your ideas
   - ❏ Replace words with stronger words

©2022 Simplify Writing®   14

Piggybacking

If you did the idea generation foundational lesson with your students, you're already familiar with piggybacking. This organizer helps students get inspiration from other authors to come up with the topic and formatting of their writing piece. This can be used with both narrative and informational writing. In the same way that the previously mentioned research form is great to be used with picture books and other text, the piggybacking organizer works great with narrative picture books when working on creative narrative pieces.

Finished Early? Anchor Chart

This checklist can be used in the same way as the one for students who are stuck. When students are finished early, they should complete these tasks until the writing block is finished. Not only will this keep students engaged in their writing, but it will provide a natural opportunity for revision. A bookmark option is available for this organizer as well.

Sentence Starters

Choose 2–3 sentence stems for your writing type to add to your writing.

Informational/Explanatory Stems

- ❑ The important thing about _____ is...
- ❑ One way/reason/idea that...
- ❑ According to the text...
- ❑ Because of this...
- ❑ This matters because...
- ❑ Many people don't know that...

Opinion/Argumentative Stems

- ❑ When it comes to _____, most people agree that...
- ❑ Some people may believe that...
- ❑ This supports the idea that...
- ❑ This evidence suggests...
- ❑ Critics may claim...
- ❑ I firmly believe that...

Narrative Stems

- ❑ It all started when...
- ❑ Before we could _____, we had to...
- ❑ First/Next/Then/After...
- ❑ All of a sudden...
- ❑ At last...
- ❑ In the end...

©2022 Simplify Writing®   16

Narrative Elaboration Ideas

Narrative Choose a character to describe in more depth.	*Narrative* Choose a setting element to describe in more depth.
Narrative Add description that shows what a character is thinking or feeling.	*Narrative* Choose a plot event to explain in more detail.
Narrative Add dialogue to show what characters are thinking or feeling.	*Narrative* Add 2–3 sentences that show what your character(s) learned.
Narrative Add sensory details that describe how something looked, sounded, tasted, smelled, or felt.	*Narrative* Add 2–3 transition words to help your story flow better.

©2022 Simplify Writing®   17

Sentence Starters

When students finish early, you want them to focus on independent revision exercises. This is especially important for the students who do the minimum to finish quickly, whose writing often lacks elaboration. These sentence starters can help students add important details to their writing. You can print these and cut them into strips to use throughout the year. Only put out the one that matches the writing type you're working on if you think your students will get confused or overwhelmed by the whole sheet.

Elaboration Cards

This card set is another great tool to fuel further elaboration for early finishers. Laminate a few copies of these and keep them in a small bin in your writing area for students to access if they're finished early. A set can also be kept at each group if your students are seated at tables or grouped desks. Students can choose a card either purposefully or randomly and do the task on the card to improve upon their writing.

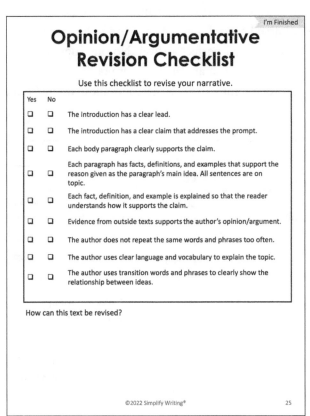

I'm Finished

Opinion/Argumentative Revision Checklist

Use this checklist to revise your narrative.

Yes	No	
❑	❑	The introduction has a clear lead.
❑	❑	The introduction has a clear claim that addresses the prompt.
❑	❑	Each body paragraph clearly supports the claim.
❑	❑	Each paragraph has facts, definitions, and examples that support the reason given as the paragraph's main idea. All sentences are on topic.
❑	❑	Each fact, definition, and example is explained so that the reader understands how it supports the claim.
❑	❑	Evidence from outside texts supports the author's opinion/argument.
❑	❑	The author does not repeat the same words and phrases too often.
❑	❑	The author uses clear language and vocabulary to explain the topic.
❑	❑	The author uses transition words and phrases to clearly show the relationship between ideas.

How can this text be revised?

 25

Revision Checklists
A simple checklist is an easy way for students to check their writing for any revisions they need to make. These checklists work best for my more advanced writers, so I tend to direct those students to this resource. Your advanced writers will still enjoy the elaboration cards and sentence starters, but they will be better challenged by using one of these rubrics to revise their writing.

File D10.1 Strategies for Early Finishers and Stuck Students

If you used all these organizers at once, your writing block would be anything but simple. Remember to keep the number of organizers to a minimum and teach your students how to access and use them properly. Using the best organizer for the situation and genre of your writing is essential, so there are a lot of options included to cover a variety of conditions.

STUDENTS FALLING BEHIND

There are always arguments in the teaching world about keeping students on the same step of the writing process versus a fluid writer's workshop. I've done both, and the simplest way to manage your writing process is to keep students on the same step. Don't get me wrong, I love the idea of the students being able to move at their own pace. However, even my advanced writers missed key elements in their writing pieces because they were going on ahead before I did my modeled mini-lesson on that step of the writing process.

In this section, I have shared some tools that these students can use to strengthen their writing pieces instead of moving on to the next step. This allows for one very polished writing piece instead of having to give them new prompts because they are ahead of the class. Revision is an extremely valuable skill for your advanced writers because they can easily rush through writing pieces at their skill level and still get a good grade. However, they need to be pushed to the next level, which means adding more complex thoughts, general improvements, and smoother transitions.

With this system in place, the remaining struggle lies with students who fall behind. This could be because they weren't able to complete the current step in time, missed school that day, or were pulled out of class. This is a problem we battle in every subject area, and there isn't a perfect answer. No one suggestion will work with all classrooms or students. It is important to note that if many students are falling behind each day, you likely need to break the steps of your writing process into smaller pieces to allow them to have enough time to complete the step.

Catch-Up Systems

System	Pros	Cons
Sending unfinished or missed work home.	Doesn't use additional class time and allows for students to work at their own pace.	Students may lose the writing piece or not complete it.
Set a "catch-up day" weekly or monthly.	Allows for students to catch up with you there to support them.	Uses already limited instructional time and may not be timely if it's monthly.
Use specials or recess time.	Allows for students to catch up with you there to support them.	Takes away from your planning and break time while also taking the student's necessary break time.
Have students quickly catch up during their independent writing time to move on to the next part.	Can be done during the writing time with you there to observe them.	Student may not catch up and may be consistently behind for the entire writing piece.

Although there's no one answer to deal with students who get behind, a combination of having a "catch-up" day and making sure that my students have enough time for each independent writing task has helped cut down on this issue immensely. Give yourself grace because this battle is not an easy one. Use recess or lunchtime as a last resort because those times offer a well-deserved break for both you and the students. Most importantly, avoid any complicated system that ends up giving you more to manage.

With your simple organizational system and procedures ready to go, it's time to start practicing them with your students. Build these procedures into your first unit and remember to model everything you want your students to do. The first unit is a learning experience for both you and your students. They're learning the procedures and expectations, while you're learning what they respond best to. Don't move on to activities like small group or writing conferences until everyone feels comfortable with what to do during independent writing time. When you're ready, later chapters will help guide you toward more differentiated learning techniques and supports for your students.

Reflect and Plan

Decide which system(s) will work for students falling behind during your writing block. How will you test these systems and adapt as you start to practice managing this issue? Which reproducible(s) will you use during your first unit for students who are stuck or finished early? How will this help you better support your students?

CHAPTER 11

Incorporate Grammar

How to incorporate grammar into the writing block may be the most hotly debated topic of all. As with everything in education, there's no one way that works for every classroom. There's also not one set of skills or lessons that will work for every classroom. Finding opportunities to differentiate for your students is key to help your students learn to use new grammar skills in their writing.

It's important to note is that grammar taught in the context of writing has better outcomes than grammar taught in isolation. Just like your lessons for the writing process, anything students learn about grammar should be directly applied in their writing. One of the biggest mistakes I see being made with grammar instruction is teachers setting aside a couple of weeks to just focus on cramming in all the grammar instruction instead of having grammar be a natural part of the writing process.

Keep in mind that errors are a completely normal part of learning how to write (Weaver, 1996). Instead of being frustrated about grammatical or spelling mistakes, we should see them as a way to help our students grow. Although repeated errors in a writing piece can be frustrating, they can also give us insight into which strategies or rules our students struggle with.

CHOOSING WHICH GRAMMAR CONCEPTS TO TEACH

Most state standards include a handful of grammar standards to teach throughout the year. When you're pacing out your year-long writing plan, you can see which writing units each concept naturally fits with. Don't start your year off by tackling every grammar standard in isolation just to check it off. Instead, focus on pre-planning which unit(s) students can learn about the concept during and then directly apply in their writing. Not only will your students better retain the information, but this method will be a more efficient use of your time since it fits into the writing unit you're teaching.

The grammar standards are not the only skills we need to teach, though. When you filled in your pre-assessment spreadsheet, you made a list of grammar concepts that your whole class struggles with. This Grammar Knockout List (Table 11.1, also seen in Appendix-A2) is the best tool you have for determining which grammatical concepts to focus on outside of the state standards. These concepts also have units that they naturally fit into. Some, like punctuation, fit well with any writing type. In general, focus on the most pressing issues on the top of your list. If the skill on the top of your list doesn't make sense for your first unit, make it a priority in the next.

Don't hesitate to focus on these grammar skills because they're below grade level. With limited time to fit in *any* grammar lessons, it may seem impossible to teach and practice both your grammar standards and past skills that students are still struggling with. Lack of time for differentiation is the main reason why students who fall behind struggle to catch up, especially in writing. There is very little time left in our day to teach anything outside of the on-grade-level standards, so finding quick opportunities to incorporate these skills into the lessons you're already teaching is essential.

Table 11.1

Grammar Skill	When will this unit be taught?	Date the unit was completed:	Notes:
List the grammar skills you need to cover from greatest impact to least impact and add notes as you cover each skill.			
End Punctuation	Week of 8/15	8-19	Most students scored 85% or above, updated on individual tab
Capitalization	Week of 8/22	8-26	Pull small groups to review capitalizing proper nouns
Fragments & Run-Ons	Week of 8/29	9-2	May need to reteach in small groups (Dahlia, Savannah, Julian)
Subject-Verb Agreement	Week of 9/6	9-9	Average score 82%, continue to review as needed
Compound Sentences	Week of 9/12		
Complex Sentences	Week of 9/19		
Dialogue Punctuation	Week of 9/26		
Comma Usage	Week of 10/3		
Titles of Works	Week of 10/10		
Quotation Marks	Week of 10/17		
Verb Tense	Week of 10/24		
Pronouns	Week of 10/31		
Quoting Text	Week of 11/7		

Sequence will differ from one class to the next

INCORPORATING GRAMMAR SKILLS INTO A LESSON

The most effective and efficient way to teach grammar skills is by incorporating them into your writing lesson. The more you model the skill in the context of a writing piece, the more your students will translate that skill into their own writing. This is why it's so important to include a plan for how you will integrate grammar naturally into your writing models. Ideally, these should be skills from the Grammar Knockout List on your pre-assessment that students have been taught in the past but have not mastered. However, it's also possible to use this strategy to teach students new grammatical concepts in context.

Do	Don't
• Use natural incorporation by making mistakes in your own writing or having your students help you figure out the correct way to write something during your model. • Focus on one grammatical concept consistently for several days or weeks. • Pre-plan how you want to model the concept by making changes in the teacher model. • Have students look for this concept in their own writing.	• Overwhelm your students with multiple concepts in one lesson. • Try to teach a full grammar lesson at the same time as your regular writing lesson. • Lose engagement by calling on just one student to help you with the grammar rule. • End your mini-lesson without giving students a way to identify the grammar concept in their own writing and use the tools they've learned to use it correctly.

The grammar skill can easily be carried over into student writing time. In fact, your goal should be to task students with the same grammar concept to focus on as they're completing each day's piece of the writing process. This can be as simple as adding it to their short "to-do" list for writing time. For example, if you're modeling punctuation as a part of your writing mini-lesson on writing dialogue, have students circle every punctuation mark they use in that day's dialogue. This is the best way to directly connect the grammar skill to their writing in context. You can also carry over the skill to any small groups, which is discussed more in Chapter 12.

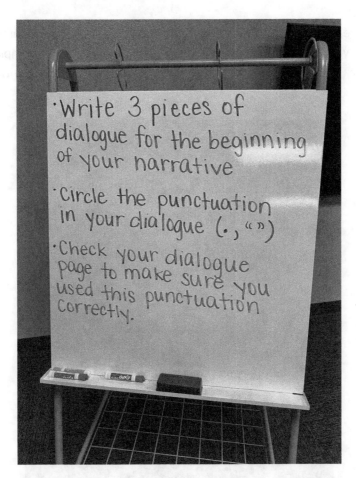

It's important to remember that your mini-lesson is still focused on a bite-sized piece of the writing process when incorporating grammar. Adding a quick opportunity or two for students to see a grammatical concept in your writing model shouldn't add more than one to two minutes to this lesson. This is the easiest way to incorporate grammar in context with very little time, so you should use this strategy as often as you can. In my following example model, you can see what this looks, and sounds like, during your mini-lesson.

Body Paragraph Organization Teacher Model

Normally, during this teacher model, you would build one of your body paragraphs using a well-written example. However, you want to incorporate the important skill of correcting fragments and run-on sentences. You can pre-plan your example to have some fragments and run-ons incorporated, as shown in the following example. During the body paragraph lesson, model this by deliberately including these errors in the model sentences. If students don't automatically correct you as you write (which is often the case when a teacher makes a mistake!), prompt them as needed.

How it sounds: "I've finished writing each part of my body paragraph, but something doesn't seem right. Do you notice anything wrong with my sentences? Yes, this first sentence isn't a complete thought. It needs a subject and a predicate. Think of how we could revise this sentence. Share with a partner how you would improve it."

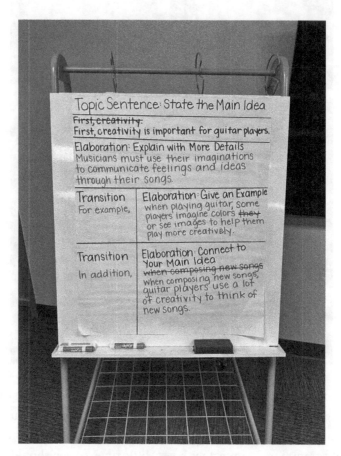

This is such a simple, yet effective, way to tackle those below-grade-level skills that your students are struggling with. Most teachers find that they need to incorporate certain skills at the top of their Grammar Knockout List repeatedly for the best results. Other teachers find that their students need more direct instruction on a concept. Direct instruction is perfectly fine, even encouraged, as long as students use the skills in concept during or after the lesson. If you have the time to do it, a standalone lesson on a grammatical concept can be very useful.

UTILIZING DIRECT GRAMMAR INSTRUCTION

Most classrooms require direct grammar instruction in addition to incorporating the skills during the mini-lesson. Two issues stop many teachers from being able to implement direct instruction lessons: time and lack of resources. Luckily, once a consistent writing block is in place, there's more time for these types of lessons. That doesn't mean that there's a lot of extra time, as the writing process can be time-consuming. However, a few dedicated grammar mini-lessons can be sprinkled in the middle of each writing unit. This makes planning and pacing very important when you need to teach the writing process while still introducing new grammar skills.

Questions to ask yourself:
- Where in my writing unit can I incorporate a grammar lesson and apply what students have learned in their writing the days after?
- How will my students use the lesson in future writing pieces?
- How can I keep my planning flexible in case I need to add a full lesson to reteach a skill?
- How can I support any students who still don't understand after my lesson?

Direct instruction gives you an opportunity to introduce a new concept to your students, but it should never be a one-time lesson. For example, you need to introduce a new and complex concept from your standards like modal auxiliaries, verbs that are used with another verb to express mood. You can model modal auxiliaries as a part of your narrative mini-lesson on dialogue, but it may be difficult for students to understand without direct instruction on what modal auxiliaries are. A lesson introducing this concept and allowing students to learn the patterns and rules is a prerequisite to practicing it in their own writing.

Week 2 Creative Narrative Pacing Example

Monday	Tuesday	Wednesday	Thursday	Friday
Planning Using Plot	Rough Draft: Setting Development	Grammar: Modal Auxiliaries	Rough Draft: Dialogue	Rough Draft: Resolution

Sample calendar with a grammatical concept built in with timing in mind. This is not a schedule for a full writing unit.

Since many studies show that teaching grammar in context outperforms standalone lessons, we have to consider how to use our direct instruction in a way that gives it context. The best way to do this is to use it in student writing immediately and continuously. This is why timing is so important. If you teach a lesson on modal auxiliaries and then move on to the next skill before students can use it in their own writing, you're unlikely to see them use the skill correctly in the future. If students immediately use it to improve their current writing piece, you're going to see a better understanding of the concept.

So, what does this actually look like?

Wednesday: The teacher defines modal auxiliaries and what the rules are for using them. Students then get to try writing their own sentences using them correctly.

Name: _Dara_   Date: _9/24_

Modal Auxiliaries

Directions: Change the mood or tone of the sentences below by rewriting them with a modal auxiliary.

	Original Sentence	New Sentence
1	I thought about going to the park.	Will I go to the park?
2	I asked my mom for some money.	I might ask my mom for some money.
3	I ran a nine-minute mile during the mile test in PE today.	I can run a nine-minute mile during the mile test.
4	I wondered about the weather forecast for our field trip tomorrow.	It may rain on our field trip tomorrow.

Directions: Use the modal auxiliaries in the box to write a paragraph on a topic of your choosing. Make sure that you use multiple options and follow the rules of modals. You do not have to use all the options in the box.

can	will	may	could	would
should	might	must	can	have

I may audition for the school play. I could sing my favorite song or I might sing my best song. I must be sure to do my best and work hard. Could I have a chance at getting a role?

Thursday: The teacher does the mini-lesson on dialogue from the writing unit. While teaching dialogue, modal auxiliaries are mentioned, and examples are given as the dialogue examples. Then, students are tasked with using modal auxiliaries while writing their own dialogue.

Using Grammar in Context
Sample Activity

After using direct instruction on Wednesday to teach about modal auxiliaries, adapt Thursday's writing lesson on dialogue practice to include modal auxiliaries in the student examples. Point these out as students practice rewriting each line of dialogue. Then, encourage students to use at least 2 modal auxiliaries as they continue to add dialogue to their own narratives.

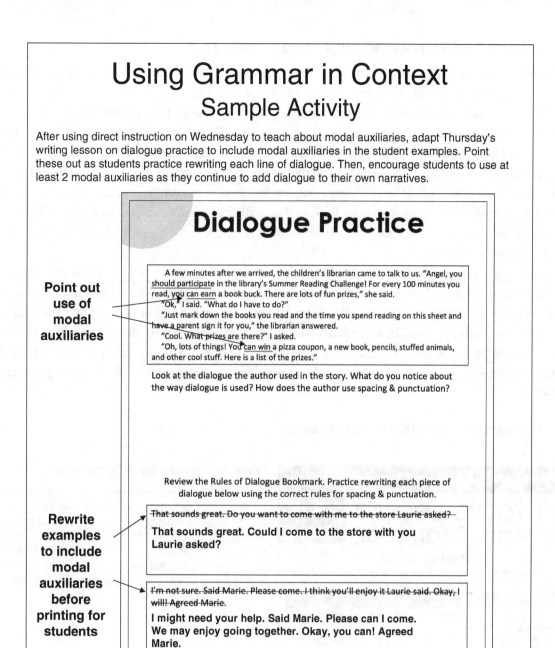

Point out use of modal auxiliaries

Dialogue Practice

A few minutes after we arrived, the children's librarian came to talk to us. "Angel, you should participate in the library's Summer Reading Challenge! For every 100 minutes you read, you can earn a book buck. There are lots of fun prizes," she said.

"Ok," I said. "What do I have to do?"

"Just mark down the books you read and the time you spend reading on this sheet and have a parent sign it for you," the librarian answered.

"Cool. What prizes are there?" I asked.

"Oh, lots of things! You can win a pizza coupon, a new book, pencils, stuffed animals, and other cool stuff. Here is a list of the prizes."

Look at the dialogue the author used in the story. What do you notice about the way dialogue is used? How does the author use spacing & punctuation?

Review the Rules of Dialogue Bookmark. Practice rewriting each piece of dialogue below using the correct rules for spacing & punctuation.

Rewrite examples to include modal auxiliaries before printing for students

That sounds great. Do you want to come with me to the store Laurie asked?

That sounds great. Could I come to the store with you Laurie asked?

I'm not sure. Said Marie. Please come. I think you'll enjoy it Laurie said. Okay, I will! Agreed Marie.

I might need your help. Said Marie. Please can I come. We may enjoy going together. Okay, you can! Agreed Marie.

©2019 Simplify Writing®
Updated 2022

51

5th Grade Personal Narrative Unit, Day 8

Friday and Beyond: Students receive different tasks with modal auxiliaries built in, from brief practice activities to natural incorporation in the teacher models and student writing time.

These grammar lessons don't always need to be planned in a way where students are using them to create new writing. You can also plan them in a way where you use the lesson to have students make revisions in their writing. One of the common concepts on the top of the Grammar Knockout List is correcting fragments and run-on sentences. A direct lesson on fragments and run-ons can be given in the middle of a writing piece, and students can be tasked with identifying and revising fragments and run-ons in their own writing.

WHAT DIRECT GRAMMAR INSTRUCTION LOOKS LIKE

Much like our lessons on the writing process, modeling is very important. When you teach a grammar mini-lesson, it's important to use the same methods as you do for your bite-sized lessons during the writing process. This translates to you teaching a short, focused lesson, then your students getting practice directly after.

Where direct grammar instruction differs from your writing process mini-lesson is in future practice sessions. On Day 1, you'll teach the grammar mini-lesson and then students will do one to two practice activities related to the lesson. Complete these activities in whole or small groups, so that students have scaffolding as they learn the skill. If you only have one day for the direct lesson and practice, you'll continue to the next step in your writing process the following day, adding the skill to student to-do lists when writing and editing their pieces. If students don't use the skill in their own writing immediately and consistently, they are unlikely to retain it.

If you do have time for further practice, you can focus on the grammar skill for a few additional days. Some teachers build this additional practice into a time of the day when they have just a few minutes to fill, instead of using the entire writing block. While you'll scaffold it on the first day, slowly take the scaffolding away as your students practice. The second day, your students may be more comfortable working on the skill in their groups. The third day, they may be able to do it in partners. And the last day, you can have them practice it independently. You can even provide a formative assessment to see where students are at with the skill.

 D11.1 Fragments and Run-On Sentences Lessons

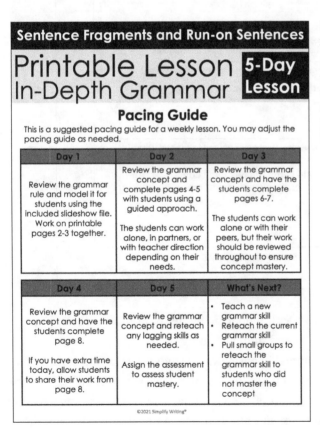

Printable Lesson In-Depth Pacing Guide

This guide gives a general overview of a multi-day lesson. Many teachers only use Day 1 if time is limited and they're focusing more on integrating the skill into current writing lessons after teaching it. If your students need more explicit practice, Days 2–5 cover using additional practice pages. This full unit is included in the resources for the book, so you can try it in your own classroom.

Sentence Fragments and Run-on Sentences

Rules: Complete sentences are sentences that contain a complete thought and include a subject (noun) and a predicate (verb). Sentence fragments and run-on sentences are common errors. If you find a fragment or run-on in your writing, you can correct it by turning it into a complete thought.

Sentence Fragments	Run-on Sentences
<u>Definition:</u> Sentence fragments are sentences that do not contain a complete thought, or incomplete sentences.	<u>Definition:</u> Run-on sentences are sentences that contain more than one complete thought without a punctuation mark to separate them.
<u>Examples:</u> 1. Birthday party at 3 pm. 2. Pizza, chips, and cake. 3. Open presents.	<u>Examples:</u> 1. Antioch MS and Crane MS competed in the Lego competition and they were very talented. 2. The Antioch team built a robot that could go up and down a ramp and they won second place and the Crane team built a robot that could dig a hole and they won first place.
<u>Corrected Examples:</u> _____ _____ _____ _____ _____	<u>Corrected Examples:</u> _____ _____ _____ _____ _____

©2021 Simplify Writing®

Day 1: Teach the Rules and/or Patterns – Sentence Fragments and Run-On Sentences

Use your 10- to 15-minute mini-lesson time to teach students any rules or patterns they need to know. For this unit, we define and give examples of both sentence fragments and run-on sentences. Model using the skill or correcting a grammatical error with several examples. During our lessons on the writing process, I encourage teachers to avoid note-taking and instead focus on participation. With the grammar lessons, students should be a part of the process correcting the examples, but they should also have their own paper to write on to keep with other grammar notes for future use of the grammar skill in their own writing.

Sentence Fragments and Run-on Sentences

Have you ever heard the saying, "April showers bring May flowers", it is true. There are two types of flowers annuals and perennials, annuals last for one season and perennials will grow back every year if you take good care of them. Make your garden beautiful.	Discuss: How can you correct the fragments and run-ons in this passage? _____ _____ _____ _____
Planting a vegetable garden. A great way to stay healthy. Cucumbers, zucchini, beans, and peas grow on vines and tomatoes and peppers grow on bushes. You can plant seeds in the soil water them and in a few months, you can make your own salad straight from your garden.	Discuss: How can you correct the fragments and run-ons in this passage? _____ _____ _____ _____
Roses come in many different colors and varieties. Tea roses, damask roses, moss roses, and cabbage roses they can be pink, yellow, peach, and more. Represent love and friendship.	Discuss: How can you correct the fragments and run-ons in this passage? _____ _____ _____ _____

©2021 Simplify Writing®

Day 1: Practice the Rules and/or Patterns – Sentence Fragments and Run-On Sentences

Practice should always come directly after the instruction so that students get a chance to apply the skill. You can use one or two grammar practice pages to do this, or you can use student exemplars.

I suggest using any practice in whole or small groups instead of as individual "quiet work." In this unit, you'll use group or partner discussion so that students can get practice applying this skill with a lot of support.

Sentence Fragments and Run-on Sentences

Cut out the sentences below the line and glue them into the correct columns below.

Complete Sentences	Fragments	Run-on Sentences

Cut out the pieces below.

Have you ever wished you were inside a video game I think it would be awesome if that happened.	My neighbor's dog was missing for three days, but we finally found her near the local park.	Finished practicing for the talent show.
Even though Derrick knew better than to disobey his mom.	My sister's friends are coming over on Sunday they are so loud.	Turn out the lights and lock the door when you leave.

©2021 Simplify Writing®

Sentence Fragments and Run-on Sentences

Choose the option below that includes only the complete sentence(s).

1
A) Since I was five years old, I have always wanted to compete in the Olympics.

B) Since I was five years old. I have always wanted to compete in the Olympics.

C) Since I was five years old, I have always wanted. To compete in the Olympics.

D) Since I was five years old, I have always wanted to compete. In the Olympics.

Choose the option below that includes only the complete sentence(s).

2
A) Jamie was excited about the weekend. Because she was going to a water park with her cousin.

B) Jamie was excited about the weekend because she was going to a water park. With her cousin.

C) Jamie was excited about the weekend because she was going to a water park with her cousin.

D) Jamie was excited. About the weekend because she was going to a water park with her cousin.

Choose the option below that includes only the complete sentence(s).

3
A) If you want to make the best possible grade on your assignment, edit and revise your writing this will make your work easier for your reader to understand.

B) If you want to make the best possible grade on your assignment, edit and revise your writing. This will make your work easier for your reader to understand.

C) If you want to make the best possible grade on your assignment. Edit and revise your writing this will make your work easier for your reader to understand.

D) If you want to make the best possible grade on your assignment, edit and revise your writing, this will make your work easier for your reader to understand.

©2021 Simplify Writing®

(Optional) Day 2+: Review with Scaffolding – Sentence Fragments and Run-On Sentences

If you choose to spend additional days on this direct unit, make sure that you do so with scaffolding. This means working in groups and providing them with immediate feedback along the way.

It's also important to vary the activities. Activities that include hands-on sorting, group discussion, and partner work are a good way to keep students both engaged and supported.

(Optional) Formative Assessment – Sentence Fragments and Run-On Sentences

After these practice activities, you can do a quick five-question formative assessment or "ticket out the door." It can be helpful to see where students are struggling to update your plans for continuing to practice this skill. If most students are doing well with the skill, you can focus more on having them search for related mistakes and correct them in their own writing. If most are still struggling, you'll likely need to model it more during your mini-lesson. If I do any sort of formative assessment on a skill, I always use it as an opportunity to update my pre-assessment spreadsheet for both individual students and our whole group Grammar Knockout List.

(continued)

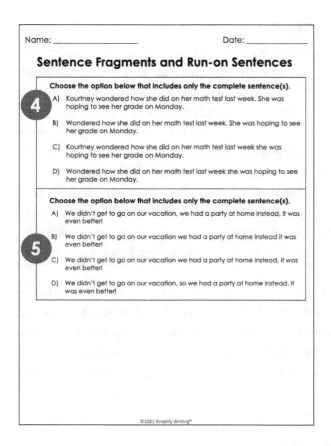

Name: _____   Date: _____

Sentence Fragments and Run-on Sentences

Choose the option below that includes only the complete sentence(s).

4
A) Kourtney wondered how she did on her math test last week. She was hoping to see her grade on Monday.

B) Wondered how she did on her math test last week. She was hoping to see her grade on Monday.

C) Kourtney wondered how she did on her math test last week she was hoping to see her grade on Monday.

D) Wondered how she did on her math test last week she was hoping to see her grade on Monday.

Choose the option below that includes only the complete sentence(s).

5
A) We didn't get to go on our vacation, we had a party at home instead, it was even better!

B) We didn't get to go on our vacation we had a party at home instead it was even better!

C) We didn't get to go on our vacation we had a party at home instead, it was even better!

D) We didn't get to go on our vacation, so we had a party at home instead. It was even better!

©2021 Simplify Writing®

Whether you choose to do a one-day lesson on the grammar skill or practice it in multiple lessons, it's important to remember that using it in the context of students' writing pieces is the most important part of your plan. This will ensure the biggest impact with your limited grammar instruction time. You can teach grammar skills for hours on end, but without them being able to apply it in the context of their own writing, you will likely continue to see them make the same mistakes when you grade their completed writing. That's extremely frustrating, so don't skip this step!

WAYS TO APPLY NEWLY ACQUIRED GRAMMAR SKILLS IN CONTEXT

1. During student writing time, challenge students to add one or two sentences that use this grammar concept correctly and underline them.

2. During student writing time, have students find correct the incorrect use of the skill. Only focus on this one skill (editing different grammar errors can be overwhelming and they may miss applying this new skill entirely).

3. Have students bring out old writing pieces and highlight both correct and incorrect use of this skill.

4. Use exemplars (sample student work) to identify correct and incorrect use of this skill.

5. Have students work with partners to identify the skill in other in-progress pieces.

WHAT TO DO IF STUDENTS STILL DON'T GET IT

If you've explicitly taught the skill and practiced it in context, but you're still finding that your students are confused or struggle to identify it in their own writing, it's not anything to panic about. It takes time for students to master these skills. One of the reasons why we're often frustrated with student grammar is that our limited writing time requires them to pick things up quickly so that we can move onto the next skill. That's an unrealistic expectation, especially for students who have been struggling with writing and grammar for years by the time they get to you. Continue to incorporate the skill into your teacher models and your independent student writing time. You should see slow and steady improvement over the weeks and months.

You obviously can't focus on every grammatical skill for weeks or months, so it's important to focus on the ones that make the biggest difference in their writing. While the occasional misuse of a comma can be annoying, something like that doesn't warrant a big instructional push for the skill. Some of the skills that I often see teachers focusing on long term are complete sentences, punctuation, capitalization, and subject-verb agreement.

If you only have a handful of students still struggling with a skill, reteaching it to them is better suited for small group time. Once your students are familiar with the expectations and comfortable using their tools to write independently, you can add in small group instruction to fill in the gaps for smaller groups of students. Take your time to master incorporating the whole group grammar skills into your lessons before you add small groups to your plate. Most teachers slowly start small groups in Quarter 2, giving themselves more time to get the basics of this system in place.

OTHER WAYS TO FIT IN GRAMMAR PRACTICE

I prefer methods that naturally fit within the writing block because they save time, but those methods focus on one skill at a time. If you want to spiral grammar skills so your students are constantly reviewing them throughout the year, there are many simple ways to do so. These ideas are meant to enrich your classroom with multiple opportunities for grammar practice in quick ways that are authentic as possible.

Spiral Daily Warm-Ups

There are often small parts of your day where you have a few minutes of transition time and need something for students to work on. The two most obvious times are first thing in the morning as students are trickling in and after lunch when they're getting settled. Use one of these times to do a quick review of the grammar skills your students have been working on.

If you use spiral grammar practice as a warm-up, make sure that the skills aren't new to your students. These should only be an extension of a grammar lesson they worked on recently, or review of a few different grammar skills they're familiar with. This review is just quick practice, so it shouldn't be graded.

These practice activities should:
- Be five questions or less.
- Be easy for students to complete in three to five minutes.
- Include a variety of question types (sentence writing, error correction, fill in the blank, underlining, etc.).
- Have a way to quickly check or review (a teacher "answer key" is helpful).

Opportunities during Reading Time

We know that reading and writing are connected. After all, everything our students read was written by someone who used the same writing skills that we teach students. Any text that your students are reading is an opportunity to discuss grammar concepts. Reading a fictional chapter book? Have students identify the dialogue and how it's formatted and punctuated. Reading a news article? Identify the important people, places, and things that are capitalized. There are opportunities around every corner for your students to see grammar in context.

Opportunities in Other Subject Areas

When students learn the skills they need to write informational and persuasive writing pieces during their writing block, they are much more confident writing about other subjects. Seeing them write about what they've learned in different subject areas with certainty about their skills is one of the major changes I saw with my students after having a consistent, dedicated writing block. Writing in all subject areas is a powerful way to show comprehension of the subject matter, but it's also a fantastic way to practice their writing skills.

As a part of writing in other subject areas, ask students to apply a specific grammar skill in their written responses. For example, when they're explaining about a historical event, tell them to write a paragraph in past tense and circle the verbs that show this happened in the past. In art, have them describe their piece using at least three adjectives. Alternatively, have them create art to represent a grammatical concept you just learned about that day. A science lesson can also incorporate grammar by having students write a step-by-step process using complete sentences with punctuation.

Reward Games

I have never been one to use candy or toys as a reward in my classroom. Instead, my students work toward fun games that we can play together as a class. Don't tell my students, but I always have an ulterior motive with these games. They're usually structured to build relationships or review concepts, and often even grammar skills.

One year, my students struggled with parts of speech, and I just didn't have the time to keep reteaching it. I decided that if my students had a great week, we'd do Mad Libs together after lunch that Friday. I'd choose a student each week who had worked extra hard, and they would select which Mad Lib we did (I had quite the collection of Mad Lib books after a while). This was a fun way to review parts of speech, and it was something that they looked forward to each week!

Real-Life Grammar Bulletin Board

It seems like everywhere we go, we spot comically unfortunate grammatical errors. We just can't help ourselves as teachers! We can turn these situations into a learning opportunity for students. Instead of simply decorating a bulletin board and leaving it the same for months, create a functional grammar board to hang "Grammar Oopsies." You and your students can bring in examples of grammar fails that you find during your everyday life. When I've done this in the past, students (and their families) have gotten competitive about spotting and collecting them! When someone brings one in, we identify the mistake and correct it as either a warm-up activity for the day or a quick activity before the bell rings.

None of these ideas are required as a part of the writing system in this book, but it's an added bonus to enrich your day with a little extra grammar practice. If this much grammar practice overwhelms you right now, focus on incorporating your grammar instruction into your writing mini-lesson and working through skills using direct instruction as needed. You can come back to this section when you're ready for a few additional ideas. As always, I recommend that you keep it simple, and do what feels right for you and your students.

GRAMMAR FAQs

CAN I USE DIRECT WRITING INSTRUCTION EVEN IF IT'S NOT A NEW SKILL?

You can absolutely use direct writing instruction for a reteach skill! Because of the struggles we covered at the beginning of the book, there's no guarantee that students have even been taught the skill in the past. If it's a grammar skill on the top of your Grammar Knockout List that most of your students are struggling with, you can use all of the strategies from this chapter to give them both direct instruction and continued exposure to it throughout the year.

SHOULD I START BY TEACHING OUR ON-GRADE-LEVEL STANDARDS OR CATCH UP ON THE ONES ON THE GRAMMAR KNOCKOUT LIST FIRST?

It can be overwhelming to think about teaching the grammar standards for this grade level and multiple standards from past grade levels. The best thing to do is prioritize these skills based on what your class needs the most and find which units they naturally fit with. Luckily, most state standards only have a handful of new grammar skills to teach. This makes it easier to balance the required lessons with the ones your students need to fill in gaps from prior years.

WHICH ORDER DO I TEACH MY GRAMMAR STANDARDS?

There's no one order that I would recommend to every teacher. Find which units the standards naturally work with, so you can easily incorporate them in with the writing units you have planned. Pre-planning where these standards go will help you teach about it in context, and not be left trying to rush to fit it in.

HOW MUCH TIME SHOULD I SPEND ON GRAMMAR EACH DAY?

There's no right or wrong answer to this question. If you're using the strategies from this chapter, you'll likely have days where you're only spending a couple of minutes on it during your mini-lesson on the writing process, where other days you spend 10–15 minutes on an explicit lesson. It will vary quite a bit, so you won't need a separate time for grammar in your writing block.

WHAT IF WE RUN OUT OF TIME AND I HAVEN'T ADDRESSED EVERYTHING ON MY "GRAMMAR KNOCKOUT LIST"?

The Grammar Knockout List is kind of like a birthday wish list. You know you won't get everything on it, but you're excited about what you do receive. And that life-changing gift that was at the top of the list? You're really pleased about that one! We prioritize the grammar skills that are needed the most and make the biggest difference in student work by putting them at the top of the list. When our students improve with those skills, or even master them, it's cause for celebration. The remaining skills that are lower on the list would be nice to tackle, but we can only do so much with the time we have.

HOW SHOULD I ASSESS GRAMMAR?

I assess grammar in two different ways. The first is a quick assessment or "ticket out the door" if I need a quick way to get a pulse on their understanding. The second is in their writing pieces. This is where true mastery shows. The beauty of the pre-assessment spreadsheet is that you can bring up the individual section while you're grading their writing pieces and see that they struggled with complete sentences initially, but by comparison, over 70% of their sentences are correct in their current piece. That's a huge win, and a great way to show progress that may not match with the typical grade-level skills in the grade book.

HOW DO I HELP STUDENTS WHO CAN'T SEEM TO TRANSFER THE LESSON TO USING IT IN CONTEXT IN THEIR WRITING?

While many students will pick up the skill and be able to find and correct mistakes they make with it, there may still be a handful who struggle with this connection. This is where writing conferences and small groups come in.

SHOULD SPELLING BE TAUGHT AS PART OF GRAMMAR?

Spelling can sometimes overlap with grammar when teaching some skills such as verb tense. However, spelling instruction and practice lists are not generally part of teaching grammar. The best way to tackle spelling in the writing block is to teach students to use tools like a dictionary to correct spelling. Other tools you can use are word walls with images that display frequently misspelled words or content vocabulary (especially when working on a technical text). Individual word books are also a helpful tool to provide a more personalized spelling support for students.

Reflect and Plan

Look at your ELA standards and mark any that specifically address grammar skills. Write next to each one which writing unit it would fit best with. Then, do the same with the top skills from your Grammar Knockout List on your pre-assessment spreadsheet. How will incorporating these skills into the units they naturally fit into save you time and help students learn them in the context of their own writing?

PART FOUR

MEETING INDIVIDUAL NEEDS

Once you feel comfortable planning for and implementing the whole group mini-lesson system, you may find that you're ready to add more individualized support for your students. Most teachers feel comfortable doing this by the end of the first quarter, but every class is different. If your writing block is running like a well-oiled machine, it's a sign that you're ready to add more support structures for small groups of students who have different needs from the whole class as a group.

Small Group (Chapter 12): This is the preferred way to work with a handful of students who need extra reteach and practice time on a specific writing or grammar skill. To be ready to start small group with your class, your students need to be able to write autonomously and be comfortable with the tools provided for their independent writing time.

Writing Conferences (Chapter 13): Taking the time to meet with each student one-on-one can be a great time to help them set individual goals. With large class sizes and limited time, conference time needs to be optimized to make it work.

Peer Feedback (Chapter 14): My favorite way to build in natural revision opportunities is through peer feedback. This allows for students to get what they need individually without relying solely on the teacher for feedback. Not only does this free up the teacher to focus on small group differentiation, but it teaches students to be more self-sufficient by seeking information on their own. Peer feedback is a valuable tool for your students to use when they get stuck or finish early.

When you get to this point, you may have also noticed that some of your students need additional support during the writing block. In **Chapters 15** and **16**, you'll learn additional differentiation strategies for English Language Learners (ELLs) and students with specific learning disabilities. These approaches vary from simple organizers you can use to support them to additional modifications you can make to your whole group lessons.

As with the other strategies in this book, do not try to implement all these strategies at once. Choose which strategy would best support your group of students and start there. If you feel like it's working well as an addition to your writing block, you can introduce an additional approach. These strategies are meant to be used together, but starting them all at once can cause confusion and feelings of being overwhelmed in you and your students. Always make sure you take the time to focus on mastering one new skill at a time.

CHAPTER 12

Support Students through Small Group Instruction

Small group instruction is a well-known strategy used in math and reading for teaching students with varying ability levels, but it's hardly ever talked about in the context of writing instruction. The fact that the instruction requires a block of independent student work time makes it a natural fit for the writing block. Small groups are an extremely powerful tool for addressing learning needs for students who range from far below grade level to above grade level.

Small groups help to focus on shared goals and allow for more personalized learning without having to create a different lesson for each student. They also encourage skill progression since goals and lessons can be modified in real time as the students interact with you. In addition to directly reteaching concepts, a small group setting allows students to practice new skills with others who have similar goals and interests. This allows them to form deeper connections that may not have been possible with whole group instruction.

This doesn't mean that writing small group comes without its challenges. One of the main reasons teachers don't use small group for writing is that their students need constant support from them during their independent writing time. This is why it's so crucial for them to master using the tools they have for independent writing, such as checklists, the teacher model, peer support, and others. In the end, the benefits from holding a small group time during your writing block far outweigh the challenges.

REASONS TO HOLD A SMALL GROUP DURING INDEPENDENT WRITING TIME

1. As an opportunity to monitor a group of students and provide feedback directly after the mini-lesson.
2. To work on a task with three to five students who share similar goals.
3. To reteach a skill that only a few students are struggling with.
4. When teaching a small group of students how to use a new tool to help accommodate their specific needs.
5. To provide an extension activity for students who are above grade level.
6. To encourage a group of students to collaborate on a task.

PLANNING SMALL GROUP INSTRUCTION

In the beginning, small group overwhelmed me. I obsessed about grouping options and explored different material options until I was stressed about the whole process. Math small group was simple and intuitive, so why was I overcomplicating it for writing? The answer to this question goes back to our common struggles: time, lack of training, and limited materials. In addition to those problems, I was missing the specific data on learning gaps for writing that I had for math.

With the right information about your students' learning gaps, planning small groups for students is simple. There's no need for elaborate materials or excessive time investment in planning each group. By identifying specific learning goals and grouping students based on their needs from the information you've already collected, you can easily create targeted activities that provide more individualized learning opportunities for your writers.

Step 1. Choose a suitable location for your small group instruction.

Small group instruction can take place in a variety of locations, such as a dedicated table a quiet corner of the classroom, or a breakout room. When choosing a location for your small group instruction, consider factors such as the size of the space, the availability of resources, and the level of distraction. If you have a co-teacher or an instructional aide helping with small groups, an area outside of the classroom can be a good way to separate the groups. For most teachers, small group instruction takes place in a corner of the classroom.

You don't need anything fancy for your small group area. If you don't have an extra table to hold it at, you can have students sit on the floor with clipboards in an area furthest from the students working independently. Also, if you have other students working together (such as peer feedback discussion), have them meet on the further side of the classroom to reduce distractions.

Keep supplies like pencils and highlighters ready to use in your small group area. Have the supplies in a caddy if you don't have a dedicated area. Make sure to keep these supplies stocked so that you don't have to interrupt your precious small group time to track them down.

The supplies I keep in my small group area:
- Whiteboard and markers or a dry-erase board and pens
- Writing utensils such as pencils, pens, or colored pencils
- Highlighters or sticky notes
- Commonly used handouts or worksheets
- Copies of recent teacher models
- Scissors and glue for sorting activities

Step 2. Identify the learning needs of your students.

Before you can plan small group instruction, it's important to identify the specific skill gaps that each student has. This can be done through pre-assessments, observations, and discussions with students. Luckily, you already have the perfect tool for this: the individual information from your pre-assessment spreadsheet. Other skill gaps may pop up as you work with students, but your pre-assessment spreadsheet is the best place to start.

When you're looking at each individual student's section of the pre-assessment spreadsheet (Table 12.1, also seen in Appendix-A3), look for skills that only two to six students struggle with. At this point, you've likely retaught (or planned to) most of the whole group structural gaps, either during your foundational preparation or by incorporating extra whole group practice into your mini-lesson. These individual skill gaps will be your first topics for small group. As your students complete future writing pieces, you can update the spreadsheet to mark off the skills that they've mastered and add new ones. I like to plan five groups (one per day) each week, and having this up-to-date spreadsheet makes it a quick and easy process.

Let's pretend that for this example you're working on an informational unit. Although several students could use small group on dialogue punctuation, they won't be able to directly apply it to their writing since they're not working on a narrative. For this reason, we will save that skill for small group time during a narrative unit.

Table 12.1

Student Names	Stamina	Sentence Writing	Paragraph Writing	Complexity of Ideas	Grammar & Spelling (Highest Priority)
Enter student names and mark categories where the student struggles with an X. List specific grammar skills in that column.					
Abdias	X			X	dialogue punctuation
Bryce	X		X	X	punctuation, spelling
Brynn	X		X	X	short, choppy sentences, verb tense
Carlos					spelling
Chantelle	X		X	X	capitalization of proper nouns, spelling
Dahlia			X		run-on sentences, punctuation
Dara					pronoun clarity
Ethan					
Evelina	X		X	X	capitalization, short sentences
Ezra	X		X	X	end punctuation, spelling
Genesis	X		X	X	using quotation marks
Grace					
Isaiah	X	X	X	X	punctuation, spelling, capitalization
Jackson	X		X	X	capitalizing titles of works, spelling
Jayden					
Julian	X		X	X	subject-verb agreement, some run-ons
Kevin	X		X	X	commas, quotation marks, spelling
Madelynn			X		dialogue punctuation
McKynna	X		X	X	capitalization, dialogue punctuation, verb tense
Nicholas					verb tense, spelling
Olivia	X			X	quoting text - punctuation
Rowan	X		X	X	sentence fragments, capitalization, spelling
Sanjay					comma usage, pronoun use
Savannah	X	X	X	X	fragments & run-on sentences, end punctuation
Sharae	X			X	comma usage, some run-ons/fragments
Sophia				X	comma usage
Trevor	X	X	X	X	subject-verb agreement, spelling
Uriel	X		X		run-ons, beginning capitalization
Xochitl					spelling

Small Group Topics: Week 1 Example				
Monday	Tuesday	Wednesday	Thursday	Friday
Basic Sentence Writing	Spelling Skills & Tools	Basic Punctuation	Advanced Elaboration	Writing Process Support

In the beginning, most of your small group sessions will be on basic writing skills and grammar. As the year progresses, you'll find yourself branching out to cover issues you notice through observations of students during the writing process. One example is that you notice five students are struggling with the counterargument of their argumentative writing during the writing process. You may want to dedicate one of your small group sessions to reteaching the counterargument and giving these students more one-on-one support while they work on it. I like to pre-plan most of my small groups the week before and reserve Fridays for this kind of impromptu support.

It's also important to make sure you include small group lessons for your advanced writers. You won't need to meet with these students as often as your struggling writers, but it is still important that they get new strategies and support where they're at, too. Too often we let our advanced writers stay stagnant because they are meeting the standards. We have a unique opportunity during small group to challenge them to improve upon their craft, instead of them writing a draft and turning it in with little effort.

Activities to try with your advanced writers:

1. **Provide constructive feedback:** Give specific, actionable feedback on the writer's strengths and areas for improvement.

2. **Help them form a community:** Advanced writers can benefit from connecting with other students during small group and receiving support and feedback from their peers.

3. **Assign them reading:** Advanced writers can benefit from reading assigned works to gain a broader understanding of storytelling and writing techniques. Provide them with a writing piece and have them write down what they notice about the tone, voice, character development, and so on. Have them try these techniques in their own writing.

4. **Explore more advanced topics:** Introduce skills in upcoming grade levels to improve their writing abilities or go deeper on a subject (like elaboration).

5. **Provide them with resources:** Give them tools they can use during independent time to continue to improve their skills. These tools can be advanced revision questions, prompts to get them thinking, advanced content vocabulary to use, or anything else that they can use to improve their writing during independent time.

Step 3. Group students by their learning needs.

Once you have identified the specific topics you want to start with, you can determine the size and composition of your small group. Small groups can range in size from two to six students, depending on the needs of your students and the goals of your lesson. For example, you may have two students who struggle to write complete sentences. For another group, you may have six students still struggling with verb tense. Unlike small group setups in other subject areas, the group size and members of each group change from day to day. When deciding on the composition of your small group, you may also want to consider factors such as students' learning styles and personalities.

Small Group Skill Planner

Monday	Tuesday	Wednesday
Basic Sentence Writing • Isaiah • Savannah • Trevor	Spelling Skills & Tools • Xochitl • Nicholas • Jackson • Isaiah • Ezra • Carlos • Bryce	Basic Punctuation • Bryce • Dahlia • Isaiah • Savannah • Trevor
Thursday	**Friday**	**Notes**
Advanced Elaboration • Ethan • Jayden • Carlos • Grace	Writing Process Support • TBD	☐ Print and copy pages from Sentence Intervention: pre-cut pg. 8 ☐ Choose activities for Elaboration practice ☐ Review Writing folders before Friday

If it's overwhelming for you to group students based off new skills each week, an alternative way is to group students by ability level and meet with these groups more consistently. Look for patterns initially on your pre-assessment spreadsheet to see what each group of students struggled with on their initial samples. You can also group them based off writing scores from a completed unit. Some teachers do a combination of both grouping types. To do this, you will look for groups of students who share similar goals and have a consistent weekly grouping. The most important thing to remember is that the students in each group must share similar goals for it to be a productive grouping. If it's possible, have a smaller group for the students who need more one-on-one instruction.

Grouping Example for Consistent Small Groups				
Group 1	**Group 2**	**Group 3**	**Group 4**	**Group 5**
Bryce Dahlia Isiah Savannah Trevor	Xochitl Nicholas Jackson Ezra Julian Uriel	Brynn Chantelle Evelina Kevin Rowan Sophia	Abdias Genesis Madelynn McKynna Olivia Sanjay Sharae	Ethan Jayden Carlos Grace Dara

Step 4. Plan your small group lesson.

Once you have identified the individual learning needs of your students, determined the size and composition of your small group, and chosen a suitable location for your small group instruction, you need to start planning what to do during each small group. To avoid getting overwhelmed by this task, make a few notes on what activities you already have that you can repurpose for each topic. This way, you're not planning entirely new activities.

When choosing your activities, consider the following:

- **Learning objectives:** What do you want your students to learn from the small group instruction? Be specific and make sure your objectives align with the goals you have for your students.

- **Teaching strategies:** What teaching strategies will you use to engage and support your students during the small group instruction? Examples of strategies you may use include direct instruction, modeling, and guided practice.

- **Materials and resources:** What materials and resources will you need to support your students during the small group instruction? Gather these materials and examples ahead of time.

- **Next steps:** What will you have students do immediately to practice the skill?

You will likely also find yourself using some of the tools from other chapters during small group time. One of the most popular tools is the color-coding in the foundational paragraph writing lesson. This can be utilized during small group to help them build a paragraph for their own writing. It can also be used to build a paragraph on almost any topic as practice.

No two small groups will look the same. Depending on your students' needs, they'll participate in a variety of activities in the group that are designed to help them improve their writing skills. Varying the format of your small group is a great way to keep students engaged.

A small group will include one or more of the following activities:

- **Mini-Lesson:** Give a short lesson on a specific writing skill or strategy, such as how to write a strong introduction or use descriptive language.

- **Modeling:** Model for a specific skill by editing or revising a part of your writing piece in front of the students and explaining your thought process.

- **Guided Practice:** Guide the students through a writing activity, providing prompts, questions, and feedback as they practice the skill.

- **Sharing:** Have students share their work with the group for feedback and discussion based on their group's goals.

- **Goal Setting:** Discussing goal setting as a group is a great way to help students find common ground and see that they're alone in their struggles. Because you are grouping students who have common needs, it is easy to set, discuss, and record goals as a group.

Daily Organizer

Date: Monday 2/4

Lesson Objective(s): Students will be able to identify what makes up a complete sentence and revise sentence fragments in their own writing.

Student Names: Isaiah, Savannah, Trevor

Lesson Information:	Materials:
• Review anchor chart (pgs. 5-6): point out subject/predicates • Sort sentences/fragments into correct categories (pg. 8) • Have students find and highlight 2-3 sentence fragments in their writing piece. what is missing: subject/predicate? • work to revise sentence fragments using anchor chart as a guide.	Complete Sentence Intervention Unit pgs. 5-6, 8 highlighters

Session Notes:

Isaiah: still struggling; continue working with resource teacher to revise fragments
Savannah: all fragments fixed; doing better
Trevor: needed support but catching on; check in next week
-could assign digital grammar pages for Isaiah and Trevor to keep working on this skill

In Chapter 16, I give you tools to use with your English Language Learners (ELLs). If you have any ELLs, you can use these tools during small group to continue to support the lessons you're already doing in your classroom. They can be a small group lesson on their own, or they can be used in conjunction with the students' current writing piece during the group. The same goes for organizers and strategies for students with learning disabilities. Use the same tools repeatedly and often so that students can master them for use during their independent writing.

Don't overcomplicate this by planning a complex lesson for each day. That's a quick way to get burned out on small groups. Reuse as many of your current lessons as you can, breaking down the content and offering more support. You'd be surprised with how far a single activity can go when you include discussion and feedback so don't over-plan.

Step 5. Implement small group.

Now that you've planned your first week, you're ready to start filling in the individual gaps that have plagued your students' writing pieces. It may seem like a daunting task, but you'll be happy you did it in a few months when you're seeing their growth. Keep in mind that implementing small group is a learning process. You'll find yourself adjusting and making changes until your groups are running smoothly.

To get students ready for small group, first make sure the rest of the class is settled and clear on the task at hand. At this point, students should be familiar with the writing block and what is expected of them. Between my mini-lesson and small group, I like to do a quick circle around the classroom to quickly answer any questions and make sure everyone has started their writing. Have students who are in your group bring their in-progress writing to your meeting place so that you can immediately use the skill in their own writing once you've retaught and practiced it.

Start your small group by stating the goal and introducing the skill they'll be focusing on today. If you're doing a short lesson or a model, spend about five minutes on that. Then, move into asking and answering questions to check for understanding. Next, you can engage your students in practice, discussion, or collaboration. Each session will look a little bit different depending on the topic and the students in the group.

Actions Observed in Successful Small Groups:

- The students participating in group discussions, brainstorming sessions, or other interactive activities.
- The teacher providing individualized feedback and guidance to each student during group work or independent activities.
- The teacher monitoring the group's progress and making adjustments as needed to ensure that the students are meeting the lesson objectives.
- The students asking questions and seeking clarification as needed.
- The students working collaboratively to complete group projects or tasks.
- The teacher summarizing key concepts at the end of the lesson and giving students time to apply the skill in the context of their own writing.

In my opinion, the end of small groups is the most crucial. Leave at least five minutes at the end to have the students revise a part of their writing. During this time, students will change or add something that directly relates to the skill you've practiced in small group. This also gives you an opportunity to provide students with feedback and support while they apply this skill. For students who get left behind during whole group lesson, this is the time for them to get the individualized attention that they need.

Leave room in your small group for students to give and receive feedback. Too often, we focus on giving students our feedback, but we don't give them the chance to apply what they've learned by critiquing it in other students' writing. Small group is a safe place for students to both give and receive feedback from their teacher and peers and use it directly in their writing.

Last, don't panic if your students still struggle with the skill at the end of your group. You may also notice that they do well in the group, but they don't retain the skill beyond it. The amount of time it takes for a student to master a skill can vary depending on several factors such as the complexity of the skill, the student's prior knowledge and experience, the quality and frequency of instruction, and the student's individual learning style and pace. On average, it can take anywhere from several weeks to several months for a student to master a skill, but it can take longer for more complex skills. It is important to note that mastery of a skill is a continuous process and is not necessarily a one-time event. For some students, the growth may be so microscopic that it isn't apparent at first.

Step 6. Assess and adjust.

As with any teaching strategy, it's important to continuously assess and adjust your small group instruction to ensure it is meeting the needs of your students. Use observation and formative assessments, such as exit tickets, quick writes, and discussions, to gauge your students' understanding and progress. Self-assessments are also a good tool for some students. If you find that your students are struggling with a particular concept, adjust your groups to provide additional support or clarification.

As students grow as writers, it's important to keep skill progression in mind. We usually think of skill progression when reviewing state standards from one grade level to the next, but each student has their own individual skill progression timeline. Each time a student becomes proficient in a skill, they have another skill to work on that builds off it. One simple example is the progression from single words to sentences, and then eventually to building a paragraph. This is a simplified skill progression, but one we often focus on as students grow in their abilities. A simple way to keep track of how students develop with these skills is by updating, or adding to, your pre-assessment spreadsheet.

Writing Skill Progression: Organization

1. Student learns to write simple sentences and create stories using pictures and illustrations.

2. Student learns to write simple sentences and begins to understand the basic elements of a story, such as characters and a plot.

3. Student continues to develop their writing skills by learning to write longer sentences and begins to understand how to organize their writing into paragraphs.

4. Student learns to write clear and detailed paragraphs, with a clear topic sentence and supporting sentences. They also begin to understand how to include transition words and phrases to connect their ideas.

5. Student learns to write multi-paragraph compositions, including personal narratives, informative texts, and opinion pieces. They also begin to understand the importance of revising and editing their writing.

6. Student continues to develop their writing skills by learning to write more complex compositions, including research reports and persuasive essays. They also learn to use more sophisticated sentence structures and vocabulary.

SETTING GOALS AND RECORDING GROWTH

Not only is it helpful to keep track of individual student progress when you're filling out report card comments, it also allows you to measure real growth in the students who are below or above the grade-level standards. Some of your students may never see an increase in their grades if measured on the same standards as other students. Not seeing a change reflected in their writing grade can be discouraging to both the student and the teacher. Keeping track of specific growth is an important piece of any equitable grading strategy.

The simplest way to keep track of your students' goals and growth is by adding it to your data-tracking spreadsheet. In the digital downloads for this book, you'll already find this set up for you under the "Student Goals" tab of your pre-assessment spreadsheet (see Table 12.2). Keep track of the skill each student is working on in small group, and write progress notes each time you meet with them.

Table 12.2

Student Names	Focus Skill	Progress Notes	Date Mastered
Abdias	punctuating dialogue correctly	small group 10/22: reviewed rules of dialogue, practiced dialogue revisions check-in 10/29: using dialogue bookmark during ind. writing time small group 11/18: making progress	
Bryce	writing a complete paragraph	small group 10/20: modeled parts of paragraph, cut/paste activity--still struggling with organization small group 10/28: worked on paragraph revisions, doing much better!	11/23
Brynn	writing longer sentences	small group 10/23: combining sentences activity--able to easily create compound sentences 11/3 highlighted choppy sentences and working to revise	11/30
Chantelle	writing a complete paragraph	small group 10/20: modeled parts of paragraph, cut/paste activity--doing okay with support small group 10/28: worked on paragraph revisions, needs more practice *assigned highlighting activity	
Dahlia	using correct endmarks	forgetting question marks--ongoing--circle end mark at end of every sentence and check it 11/16 conference: making progress only 2 errors	12/7

Student Names	Focus Skill	Progress Notes	Date Mastered
Abdias			
Bryce	using commas correctly	12/6 reviewed comma rules during writing conference--working to revise essay	
Brynn	creating complex sentences	small group 12/4: What makes a complex sentence? Practiced with examples small group 12/13: still struggling to apply in context	
Chantelle			
Dahlia	correcting run-on sentences	conference 12/9: circled run-ons, going to fix during revision process--share with a partner when done	

File D5.1 Pre-Assessment Spreadsheet Sample

Setting goals and tracking growth shouldn't be limited to the teacher's records. By having clear goals, students can see exactly what they're working for and that it's attainable with small, gradual steps. Tracking growth gives students a better idea of whether they are making progress toward those goals and provides powerful motivation for continuing with difficult writing tasks.

Tracking progress can lead to self-motivation that is crucial for students to succeed in both school and home settings. Many research studies have emphasized the importance of involving students in setting their own learning goals and monitoring their own progress. One example is a 1993 study of 40 fourth graders, where half received feedback and goals and the other half did not. The students with a process goal and feedback: (1) outperformed the control group on posttest self-efficacy and skills, self-efficacy for improvement, and perceived progress in strategy learning; (2) scored higher than did product goal children on posttest skill and perceived progress; (3) wrote more words per unit and judged posttest strategy use and strategy value higher than did product and general goal students; and (4) performed better on the maintenance test than did general goal children. Students who received the process goal without progress feedback scored higher on writing skill and wrote more words per unit than did general goal students (Schunk and Swartz, 1993).

With knowledge of their individual goals, and your support, students can focus on an area of growth following the skill progression. Each time they progress with a skill, they have a more difficult skill waiting for them. This ensures that students are constantly learning and growing. For younger students, this may look like a student-friendly checklist with a skill progression that you show them and mark off together as they master skills. For older students, this may mean that they independently set and track goals and journal about their progress.

Name: trevor

Student Goal Page

My goal: writing complete sentences

Today I learned a complete sentence needs a subject and a predicate. A subject is who or what the sentence is about and a predict tells what the subject dose.

I will use this in my writing by checkin each paragraph to make sure that my senteces all include a subject and a predicat. I will highlight any sentence fragment so I can revise them.

Tools I will use to meet my goal:
complete sentence anchon chart checklist
Highlighter

©2023 Simplify Writing®   4

Small group is one of the best ways to reinforce goal setting and tracking growth. You may not have the time to meet with students individually to track goals, but you can use a portion of small group time to update their goals and monitor progress. When a student can put a strategy in place without needing your support, it's time for them to move onto more challenging work or a new goal (Serravallo, 2021). This is one of the reasons why I always suggest small group before getting into writing conferences. Many teachers find that small group is what they truly needed for their students to get feedback and individualized support without the time requirements for conferences.

Skills I'm Working On

Name: *Trevor*	
Skill	**How to Practice This in My Writing**
writing complete sentences Date Mastered: *10/30*	*Check each sentence for a subject and a predicate.*
writing compound sentences Date Mastered: *12/14*	*Using conjunctions to combine sentences (FANBOYS)*
writing more complex sentences Date Mastered: *2/12*	*Adding elaborative details* *Using subordinating conjunctions to combine sentences*

10

 File D12.1 Small Group Planning Pages

WRITING SMALL GROUP FAQs

HOW MANY SMALL GROUP SESSIONS SHOULD I DO EACH DAY?

The reason why I used one session as an example in this chapter is that most teachers do one small group session each day. Each small group takes about 15–20 minutes. If you have extra time in your block, you may want to try a few one-on-one writing conferences or a group conference.

SHOULD I SEE EACH STUDENT EQUALLY?

Unless you're doing consistent grouping for your small group, it's unlikely that you'll see every student for the same number of sessions. When you group by topics, there may be a few students who are in more than one session. Don't stress over seeing each student equally. Instead, focus on how you can support each student in the way they need.

WHAT IF THE SAME STUDENTS STRUGGLE EVERY DAY?

This is a common issue during independent writing time. While it's sometimes temping when a student is always stuck or off task, it isn't feasible for a student to be in small group every day. Not only would it overwhelm them with too many new skills and tasks, but it wouldn't give them the time they need to *actually* write. This means that you need a solid plan in place for what to do for these students. This may be a writing buddy or support tools they can use to write independently. Even if their writing is completely off base, it's better than no writing at all.

HOW DO I HELP STUDENTS WHO FINISH EASILY AND DON'T REALLY NEED ANY HELP?

These students tend to be early finishers because they don't *have* to revise to get a passing grade. Unfortunately, this leads to a lot of them becoming stagnant. They usually go unnoticed because they can get by easily, or they end up helping other students. It's imperative that we have a small group for these students to introduce more advanced skills or give them the tools they need to really improve their writing. Small group for advanced writers also helps students form a community that they may call on in the future for feedback.

WHAT IF THE SKILL YOU'RE WORKING ON DOESN'T FIT IN WITH WHERE THEY'RE AT IN THE WRITING PROCESS DURING THEIR INDEPENDENT WRITING TIME?

It's important to make sure that you have a solid plan for students to use the skill in their writing immediately. If you're working on narrative writing, reteaching a skill like quoting a text wouldn't be very meaningful. Choose your group topics based on what type of writing you're working on. If students are in the planning phases for a new unit, that would be a good time to meet with students who need help on idea generation and organization. Once you move into body paragraphs, you have more room to apply grammar and structure skills.

WHAT IF THEY GET BEHIND ON THEIR WRITING PIECE BECAUSE THEY WERE PULLED FOR SMALL GROUPS?

While other students are working on the part of the writing process covered during the mini-lesson, the students in small group are missing that time. The best way to combat this is to connect the topic you're addressing with the part of the writing process where they'll use it the most. When that's not possible, you'll want to implement one of the "Catch-Up Systems" section in Chapter 10, such as having an extra catch-up day built in every once in a while. There isn't a perfect answer, but it is worth figuring out what works for your class so that your students can get the help they need.

Reflect and Plan

Look for students with similar writing goals, then create your groups for the first week of small groups. Plan a general outline of what you'll work on for each group. Last, jump in and try it! Come back to reread this chapter at the end of your first week and adjust as needed.

CHAPTER 13

Provide Individualized Feedback through Writing Conferences

My first experience with writing conferences was a poor one. I had a class of 29 students and a predictably short writing block. It wasn't long after beginning the conferences that I gave up on the idea all together. I felt like I was resigned to teaching each lesson, then grading the work students rushed through without making any changes. I felt like I didn't have the time or resources to give 29 students individual feedback.

Looking back, there were obvious issues with how I had writing conferences set up. I don't blame myself for giving up at the time. I was following the traditional structure for writing conferences: have a student come back and read their entire draft to me, then show them every mistake I found. I was the personal editor for 29 students with only 15 minutes a day to do it. Not only was it unsustainable, but my students didn't really enjoy the process, either.

Writing conferences *can* be a valuable tool for helping students to improve their writing skills, if done right. They provide an opportunity for individualized feedback on student writing and can also be used to address specific areas of weakness or to celebrate areas of strength. By scheduling regular conferences, providing written feedback, and using digital tools, you and your students can see and celebrate progress over time.

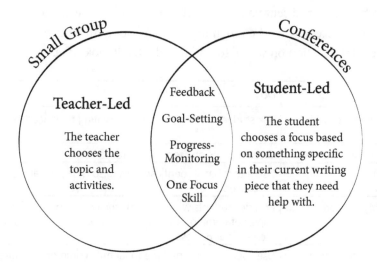

A PROCESS THAT WORKS

To consistently use conferences in your classroom, you need a system that fits into the time you have and allows for you to confer with all of your students on a reasonable timeline. For teachers who can't (or don't want to) fit in individual conferences, this may mean using a group or peer conference system. For others, it will mean quick, actionable conferences with individual students. Both strategies can be just as effective, so it's a matter of finding what works best for you and your students.

Individual Conferences

Making individual conferences work in a present-day classroom usually requires a shift in beliefs about the structure of these sessions. It may be an unpopular opinion, but writing conferences are not a good tool for extensive editing. That doesn't mean that there isn't a place for them in your classroom, though. They can be an exceptional tool for identifying common issues to reteach, helping students focus on a single goal or revision, and giving students general support during their writing.

Put aside the belief that every error needs to be fixed in the student's writing for a conference to be successful. Instead, adopt the idea that this is just one of the many ways you will support your students during the writing process. Any feedback should be delivered one part at a time, to not overwhelm the writer (Hammond, 2015). They will have additional opportunities for support when they get feedback from their peers and work with you in small group. The focus of your conference should be to establish a single goal and give them a tool or strategy to use it in their writing.

If you learn to focus in on a specific area of revision for each student, you can have a meaningful one-on-one conference in just five minutes. When you choose one clear focus, it allows for students to concentrate on one single improvement. This helps prevent the overwhelming feelings that many students get when they leave a conference with a dozen or so marks on their page. A full edit of their writing is better suited for a time other than conferring.

It may be time to train yourself to focus just on one key skill when you see so many different mistakes in their writing. When this happens, imagine how you'd perform if someone verbally told you a long list of groceries and then sent you off to the store. If you're like me, you'd be stressed the entire way there, forget half of the items, and end up with a cart full of ice cream. What if the person instead told you one thing to pick up, what aisle to find it in, and sent you a picture? There wouldn't be any anxiety about that shopping trip, and your chance for success would be much higher. Send your students off with one task to improve their writing, with clear information on where to find it and what it looks like.

Do Not	Do
Have students read their entire writing piece for you to critique.	Ask students which part of their writing they need help with.
Circle every error on their writing piece.	Give students one repeated error to correct.
Do all the talking.	Listen to what students are saying so that you can address and correct misconceptions.
Let students leave empty-handed.	Provide students with the tools they need to revise their writing piece. Keep copies of commonly used writing tools (checklists, rubrics, sentence frames, etc.) at your disposal.
Get frustrated when something you just taught isn't being applied in their writing.	Use your one-on-one time to identify common struggles that you may need to reteach.
Forget to record student growth.	Note updates next to the student's name on your recording spreadsheet.
Focus only on conventions.	Focus on style, organization, and other skills that are needed for clarity and high-quality writing.

When, Where, and How Often

Like small group, writing conferences happen during independent student writing time. In many cases, you will confer with your students in the same area as your groups with the same supplies. If there isn't enough time to do both small group and individual writing conferences during student writing time, you will need to choose separate days or weeks to confer with your students individually. This may look like reserving every Friday for group conferences or doing small groups for two weeks and then conferences for two weeks.

There's no right answer regarding how often to confer with your students. Most teachers believe it needs to be done every week to be beneficial, but that's not always sustainable. The frequency of writing conferences will vary depending on your schedule and writing goals. You may find that your students benefit from small group more, which is totally fine. Writing conferences are a tool to support your students, not something you need to do because you feel obligated to do them. Remember that there are many ways for students to get feedback and support. Schedule time to confer with your students when you think it would be the most beneficial.

During years where most of my students were critically behind in their writing skills, I found myself doing small group more than individual conferences. Conversely, when I had a class with only a handful of struggling writers, we did conferences more than small group. It's all about choosing what works best with your schedule and goals.

Many of the teachers I work with prioritize small group instruction until later in the writing piece, where they meet individually with students. They still see the writing pieces as they progress since the skill they're focusing on in groups gets directly applied in student writing. Other teachers skip one-on-one conferences all together and just do group conferring. There is no wrong combination or schedule.

Before the Conference

If you're set up for small group, you're ready to go for writing conferences, too. You have a "quiet enough" area to work with students, and commonly used writing tools (checklists, rubrics, sentence frames, etc.) at your disposal. You're familiar with student struggles from what you observed during their pre-assessment and in any units since. The only prep work to do is to help your students prepare for the conference.

A pre-conference form is imperative if you want to have a short, actionable conference. It's also a great way to set or update goals. It's time to stop having students read their entire writing piece aloud for you to critique and to start asking them where they need support the most.

For most students, this form will seem foreign, and maybe a little bit difficult. We don't ask students enough to reflect on where they're struggling. We usually go straight to pointing it out to them. This is why I always do a mini-lesson where I introduce the pre-conference form and have them discuss and share areas where they've struggled lately. The examples don't have to be writing related, they can be in a sport, at home, or in another subject. When students share, show the class what it looks like on the form to be specific and provide details in order to express their needs.

Pre-Conference Form

Name: _Madi_	Date: _10/28_

Something going well in my writing is:	I used a lot of detail.
Something that's challenging or I'm unsure of in my writing is:	Oganizing my ideas
Two specific questions I have:	1. Wich idea do I put fist 2. Spelling big words.
Feedback I received:	put most imparted idea first, use planning out line, sound out words, use dictionary to cheak.
Next Step:	find planning out line, cicle word to cheak laten

©2021 Simplify Writing®

You can find this form in your downloadable files and in the Appendix of this book.

File D13.1 Pre-Conference Form

Once students are familiar with the form, you can have them complete it prior to each conference. Put a list on the board for next day's conference so they have time to complete it at the end of the writing time. Each student should come to their conference with the form, their writing process, and a pencil.

During the Conference

During the conference, you should actively listen to the student as they share something from their pre-conference form, and then ask open-ended questions to guide the conversation toward one skill to focus on during the session. The focus will be on just one specific area of the writing, such as organization, sentence structure, or a specific grammar rule. You need to put aside the natural inclination to want to fix everything and focus on giving students a usable amount of information (Brookhart, 2017). This conversation should be quick and to the point, taking about 90 seconds in total.

When you're discussing their writing, make sure the language you're using is supportive and student-friendly. A phrase that I've adopted from Kelly Boswell (2020) is "as a reader." For example, a student comes to you saying that they don't know how to end their story. They read their ending from their draft and it's lacking a resolution. I'll say, "As a reader, I really like when the ending of a story explains what happens to all of the main characters. I was confused about what happened to the Oliver character at the end of your story. What actions and events could you add to give the full picture of what happened to him?" This helps them see that you're there to help them write a better story for their reader, which gives them purpose and motivation to make the revisions.

Skill/Goal	Strategy	Student Application
Writing a resolution that wraps up the story.	Write two or three character actions or events that will explain what happens to the character named Oliver at the end of the story.	Take the actions or events and use them to rewrite the end of your story.

The majority of time spent in the conference will be on giving the student a strategy to help them apply the skill and meet their goal. This will take about three minutes. Once the student has seen the strategy and tried it out, you'll give them a very similar next step to use their strategy in their own writing. This should be something they focus on each day during independent writing time, so make sure that you're clear that it's not a one-time use strategy.

The entire conference totals to about five minutes. When you first start, you may find yourself going over this time. If this happens, consult the previous "Do/Do Not" chart to see if there are any simple issues you can fix.

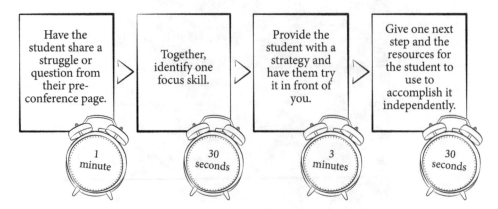

Often the most difficult part for teachers is being able match the skill-based goal with a simple strategy to use with students to meet it. A helpful strategy for students may be a process that they follow or a hint they tell themselves when encountering the skill in their writing. You may also provide a technology-based tool or paper organizer for students to use when they practice the skill.

Although this list isn't extensive, the goal and strategy lists in this book are a helpful starting point when providing your students with strategies to meet their specific goals. To find this list of common goals and strategies, flip to the Appendix. There are four pages titled *Common Student Goals & Strategies* that provide excellent examples.

You may have noticed that the goals and strategies lists include a small section for conventions. Although they are important, there is so much more to your students' writing. It's important to find a healthy balance of content skills and conventions. If we overemphasize them, we can squash the enjoyment of writing (Boswell, 2020).

In *How to Give Effective Feedback to Your Students* (2017), Susan Brookhart writes, "Feedback can lead to learning only if the students have opportunities to use it." It is imperative that you focus on one piece of meaningful feedback that they can practice directly in their writing. Once you've pinpointed the focus skill and the student has tried the strategy in front of you, send the student off to continue trying it on their own. Give them a brief "next step" to focus them on this task. This is as simple as telling them to use the exact strategy they just used in front of you, but independently in their own writing.

It is also important to provide positive feedback and to celebrate the student's strengths as you wrap up the conference. Positive feedback can also help to establish a sense of trust and rapport between the writer and the teacher, which can lead to more productive and meaningful conferring in the future. The combination of positive feedback and giving them one specific strategy will help to focus the writer's attention on specific areas of improvement, rather than being overwhelmed by an overall sense of criticism.

After the Conference

After the conference, the student should continue revising their writing based on the feedback received. They should do this by revisiting the strategy you provided them with. At their next conference, check in on this strategy and see if they're ready for a new one or need to continue to practice it.

Just like with small group, it's important to keep track of how students are progressing with their goals. Keep this information in the same place as your small group tracking. Small group and conferences both serve similar purposes, so there's no reason to track data differently or use completely different strategies with your students in each.

Group and Peer Conferences

Another way to use writing conferences in the classroom is to have students conference with each other. This can be done in small groups or one-on-one. It can be with teacher guidance or without. Peers can provide valuable feedback on each other's writing and can help students to see different perspectives on their work.

Group Conferences

During a group writing conference, writers present a piece of their work, with specific questions about it, to a small group of their peers. They receive specific feedback using their pre-conference form. The goal of a group writing conference is to help writers improve their work and gain a better understanding of the writing process in a way that's more collaborative than individual conferences.

To start a group writing conference, you will need to gather a small group of writers who share similar goals. It's important that all participants provide constructive feedback and to be open to receiving feedback from others. It may take you a few sessions to show students how to give feedback that is productive and respectful.

Before the conference, students should be given specific instructions to bring their filled-out pre-conference form, writing process, and a pencil. This will likely take place in the same small group area. However, instead of having a predetermined goal for the skill they're learning, group conferring is all about focusing on a skill that the student identifies as an issue in their writing.

During the conference, it's important that everyone listens carefully to the student sharing their questions and struggles from their pre-conference form. Then, they will share the part of their writing piece that correlates with the skill or issue. For example, if they're struggling with a thesis that's just not quite right, they'll share what they have written for it before accepting feedback.

As a part of this process, students will learn to listen and collaborate to solve problems and improve the writing of others. Part of this process is to learn how to give specific feedback. Keep a chart in your group conferring area with poor feedback and specific feedback. When you hear generalized feedback from a student, stop to write it on the chart and have them help you make it more specific. After practicing this for a while, you'll start to notice students using more specific feedback. You'll also notice some great revisions and additions from this feedback when you get their final drafts.

Poor Feedback	Specific Feedback
It's good. I like it.	I like the dialogue between the mother and daughter. It really shows me how much they love each other.
You need to write better.	Revise these sentence fragments.
You should add more details.	I think you can support your opinion in paragraph 3 better if you add a quote or another piece of supporting evidence.
You have bad spelling.	I noticed a misspelled word right here. What tools can you use to find the correct spelling?
You're missing punctuation.	I heard you pause between these two sentences, but I don't see any punctuation. You should add punctuation so that the reader knows to pause as well.

Most teachers guide their group writing conferences so they can give feedback and track progress. However, if you find that a group of students is working exceptionally well together, you can have them meet without you. This is a great way to meet the needs of your more advanced writers while working with a group of struggling writers. You can even set aside a day to have everyone confer in groups!

An added benefit to teaching students to give and receive specific peer feedback is that they can do this on their own if they need feedback when it's not their turn. Chapter 14 discusses how to set up a peer feedback system in your classroom that helps them do this in a manner that does not disrupt other students. This is a great support for students who get stuck or are finished early while you're conferring or working in a small group.

Using Digital Tools for Conferences

In addition to these methods, there are also digital tools available to help with writing conferences such as Google Docs and Microsoft Word, which allow teachers and students to collaborate on a document in real time and make changes and suggestions as they go. It's important to remember that if students are using these tools, it should still be focusing on specific feedback, not just making edits. If they only use these tools to help each other edit, it's unlikely that you'll see the high-quality content that comes from specific feedback.

WRITING CONFERENCES FAQs

HOW OFTEN SHOULD I MEET WITH EACH STUDENT?

Every classroom is different. Choose a schedule to try that is realistic and consistent. It may take a couple of months to find a good balance with both small group and conferences.

WHAT IF STUDENTS ARE JUST STARTING A WRITING PIECE WHEN IT'S THEIR TURN TO CONFER?

Every part of the writing process is a good part to get feedback and work toward individual goals. When you're focusing on specific feedback instead of editing an entire writing piece in your conferences, you'll find that takes the pressure off what students need to have accomplished before conferring with you.

WHAT IF A STUDENT DOESN'T HAVE HELPFUL CONTENT ON THEIR PRE-CONFERENCE FORM OR DIDN'T FILL IT OUT?

Some students are better at self-reflection than others, so it's common for some students to need extra support to learn how to reflect on their writing piece. For the students who never see anything to revise or edit in their pieces, learning how to self-reflect is going to be beneficial in many ways. It may be challenging to get them to this place, but keep at it by asking prompting questions to guide them to find an area they can improve in.

SHOULD THE STUDENT READ ALOUD OR SHOULD I READ THE WRITING MYSELF?

Always have students keep ownership of their writing by reading aloud the part you're focusing on. Remember not to have them read their entire piece aloud, as it takes too long and can put the focus on correcting the entire piece. Instead, have the student read aloud specific sentences or sections that relate to their goal.

SHOULD I MAKE NOTES RIGHT ON THE STUDENT'S WRITING?

Continuing the theme of student ownership, it's important to have students write the notes they need and make changes in their writing. You can provide a sticky note for them to write their "next step" on and place over the part of their writing to focus on (if applicable), or use the pre-conferencing form to note this information.

HOW MANY THINGS SHOULD I ADDRESS IN ONE CONFERENCE?

Focus on just one skill. It's tempting to point out minor errors you see, but too much input will make it difficult for the student to remember the important directions you gave regarding their goal.

SHOULD I NOTE EVERY SPELLING CORRECTION?

Only have students make spelling corrections if you have the student working on a specific strategy for spelling as your one skill-based goal.

WHAT IF I CAN'T GET TO EVERY STUDENT DURING A WRITING UNIT?

As long as students have other ways to get feedback and work toward their individual goals (small group, peer feedback, etc.), it's okay if you don't confer with every student during each unit.

WHAT IF I CAN'T MAKE INDIVIDUAL CONFERENCES FIT INTO MY SCHEDULE?

It's totally fine to skip individual conferences to focus on a form of individualized instruction that works better for you. You may find that group conferences and/or small group are easier to manage and better support your students with their goals.

HOW DO I CHOOSE BETWEEN INDIVIDUAL AND GROUP CONFERRING?

I always recommend trying both conference setups to see what works best. Teachers with shorter writing blocks tend to gravitate toward group conferences for better efficiency. Group conferences help students learn how to collaborate to improve their writing, so there's nothing wrong with choosing them instead of individual conferences.

WHAT IF THEY GET BEHIND ON THEIR WRITING PIECE BECAUSE THEY WERE PULLED FOR SMALL GROUPS?

Each student will miss about seven minutes out of their independent writing time to confer with you. This disruption won't cause issues for all students, but it can be helpful to work on the skill as a part of what they're working on independently. This gives them a direction to take when they get back to their seat, and sometimes even some time to work on it during the conference. For students who struggle to get back on task if interrupted, it's better to confer with them last.

Reflect and Plan

Determine which type of writing conferences you want to start with (group or individual). Create a schedule of the days and times each month when you want to focus on conferring with students. Decide if you want to try conferences every week or switch off by doing small groups for a week or two and then switch to conferences. If you created a weekly schedule for small groups, incorporate conferences into it for future weeks.

CHAPTER 14

Integrate Peer Feedback Systems

As is discussed in prior chapters, feedback is an important aspect of the writing process. A few benefits of peer feedback include increased student engagement and motivation, improved quality of student work, and increased student understanding of the learning goals (Brookhart, 2017). Structuring time for peer feedback allows writers to receive constructive criticism and valuable insights on their work. By getting feedback from others, writers can gain a different perspective on their writing and identify areas that need improvement. This can include issues with conventions, sentence structure, organization, and overall flow.

Peer feedback is often missing from classrooms because the quality is considered low compared to adult feedback. However, feedback from peers helps writers to build a sense of community and camaraderie among their peers. It allows them to share their work with others, receive feedback, and give feedback to others, which can help to create a sense of shared ownership and responsibility for the writing process. This can be especially beneficial for writers who struggle to write independently and require feedback more often than the teacher can provide.

Teaching students how to give peer feedback can also help to promote self-reflection and self-awareness. When students are providing feedback to their peers, they are also reflecting on their own work and understanding the areas where they need to improve. This can be a valuable learning experience that allows students to take more ownership of their own learning process.

Additionally, peer feedback can help writers build self-confidence and get motivated. By receiving positive feedback on their work, they can gain a sense of validation and encouragement to continue working on their writing. Constructive criticism can also help writers to identify specific areas of improvement and motivate them to work on those areas. Overall, peer feedback is an essential tool for students to improve their work and stay motivated throughout the writing process.

Ways to Encourage Quality Peer Feedback:
- Teach students the importance of being specific and detailed in their feedback. Instead of simply saying "I liked it" or "I didn't like it," students should be taught to identify specific parts of the writing that they liked or didn't like, and to explain why.
- Emphasize the importance of being constructive and respectful in their feedback. Students should be taught to provide feedback that is honest and helpful, rather than simply criticizing or tearing down the work of their peers.
- Model the process of giving feedback by providing examples and asking students to give feedback on your own work. This can be a good way to demonstrate how to give specific, constructive, and respectful feedback.
- Encourage students to give feedback on the content, organization, and conventions of the work and not the person; this will help them to focus on the writing rather than the writer.
- Teach students to give and receive feedback in a positive and supportive atmosphere, where they feel comfortable and safe sharing their work and their thoughts.

- Encourage students to get feedback not only on the finished product, but also during the writing process, to help them improve as they go.
- Remind students that feedback is a process and that it takes time to improve as a writer, and that feedback is an important tool to help them on that journey.

OPPORTUNITIES FOR PEER FEEDBACK

Even with a short writing block, there are many occasions for peer feedback. The best opportunities are ones that happen naturally and don't need additional time taken out of the block. However, it can be beneficial to plan days during your writing unit to teach students how to conduct peer feedback as a part of a structured lesson. It's important to do this before you start having students give feedback on their own, so you can make sure that it is a helpful experience when they do.

You can teach students how to give feedback at any time during the writing block, not just at the end when the rough draft is complete. Too often, we save feedback until the end during a single revision and editing lesson. It's not a bad thing to use revision and editing at the end of your units, but it's important that students also receive feedback and revise through the entire writing process.

Building Peer Feedback into a Unit

Monday	Tuesday	Wednesday	Thursday	Friday
Elements of Informational Writing	Brainstorming	Research	Planning: Organization	Peer Feedback Opportunity

In this example, students have started to organize the information from their background knowledge and research on the topic. This can be a lot of information to sort, so an opportunity for peer feedback before moving onto the rough draft will be very helpful. Setting aside an entire block for this allows for you to also teach students how to give and receive quality feedback. This would be a great opportunity for the peer feedback lesson (download file D14.1), if you haven't given it already.

Another great opportunity for peer feedback is when you have a student who is "finished" early. Receiving feedback and revising their writing is better use of their time than doing free choice work or reading a book. There's always something students can do to improve their work, but it can be difficult to determine what that is without feedback.

The best way to take advantage of this opportunity is to set up a *Peer Feedback Station*. This is an area of your room where students can meet to discuss their writing when they need it. When a student gets to the station, they should start filling out a feedback form. This helps pinpoint exactly where the student needs help, so their partner can provide quality feedback.

Once two students are at the station and ready, the feedback session can start. The student who was there first will share what they wrote on their feedback form. They may share something like, "I finished my introduction paragraph, but I think my hook is boring." This will prompt their partner to help them come up with ideas to revise their hook. If they were unable to come up with anything to ask for help on, they can read their writing aloud while their partner asks clarifying questions. A clarifying question is a great way to express that they don't quite have all the details to understand that part of the writing, so the writer should use their answer to the question to add or change parts of their writing for clarity.

At the end of the station, both students will return to their independent writing areas and immediately use the feedback to revise their writing. If the writing block ends before they can do this, they should keep their feedback form with their writing piece and do it as soon as possible the next day.

The same structure works for students who are stuck. Instead of sitting around while they wait for the teacher to have an opportunity to "unstick" them, they can work with a peer who needs feedback as well. There's no separate station for these students. They'll meet with peers who are finished early, stuck, or just needed a break from writing to talk something through. Being able to get feedback on-demand is such a valuable tool for all students.

TEACHING STUDENTS HOW TO CONDUCT PEER FEEDBACK SESSIONS

It's important to teach students how to give and receive feedback in order to promote a positive and supportive learning environment. When students are equipped with the skills and strategies needed to give effective feedback, they can provide their peers with the support and guidance they need to improve their work. This will foster a sense of collaboration and teamwork, which is especially beneficial to the writing block.

To provide effective feedback, students must be able to analyze and evaluate the work of their peers, and then express their thoughts and ideas in a clear and concise manner. It requires a level of self-reflection and self-awareness. These are not skills that all our students have. Clearly teaching students how to give peer feedback will provide them with the opportunity to learn and practice these skills.

It's also important to note that teaching these skills can help to promote diversity and inclusivity in your classroom. When students are taught how to give feedback in a constructive and supportive manner, they are less likely to be judgmental or dismissive of the work of their peers. This will help to create a learning environment where all your students feel comfortable sharing their work and receiving feedback, regardless of their background or experience.

🔗 File D14.1 Peer Feedback Lesson

Giving Great Feedback

Great feedback includes **specific** information about how to improve the work.

Feedback Sources

Peers
Family
Teachers
Friends

Ask Yourself:
- ☐ What information can be elaborated on to make this piece better?
- ☐ How can this piece of work be taken to the next level?
- ☐ What errors do I see repeated throughout the piece?

Poor Feedback	Great Feedback
It's good. / I like it.	I like the dialogue between the mother and daughter. It really shows me how much they love each other.
You need to write better.	Revise these sentence fragments.
You should add more details.	I think you can support your opinion in paragraph 3 better if you add a quote or another piece of supporting evidence.

©2019 Simplify Writing® Updated 2022 1

Feedback Form

Date: 11-5-21   Writing Piece: "A Lasting Impact"

Questions I have:	☐ Does my introduction provide enough background information for the reader? ☐ What kinds of details should I add in this body paragraph to better support my main idea? ☐
Feedback:	It would help if you added a sentence with the definition of the word "entrepreneur" in case the readers don't know what that word means. You could add some evidence with data that shows how many people have participated in the program

What I'm doing with this feedback:

I am going to add the definition of "entrepreneur" to my introduction to give more background information to my reader. I will also do some more research to find the percentage of students who have taken part in the residence program

©2019 Simplify Writing® Updated 2022 4

Introduce Peer Feedback

Create an anchor chart with your students about giving and receiving great feedback. During this lesson, students will learn:

- Whom to get feedback from.
- Questions to ask themselves when giving feedback.
- What great feedback looks like.

This organizer should be kept hanging in your room, and students should reference it any time they are giving feedback.

Focus the Feedback

To further focus the process, students need to know how to use a feedback form for their own writing. Model using this form to get feedback for your own writing. Then, ask students the questions and write down the feedback they provide. The last step is to decide what you're going to do with the feedback.

Practice using this form by building peer feedback opportunities into your writing block. Once students have mastered it, you can set up an autonomous peer feedback station with this form.

Feedback Form

Teacher Model

Date: _9-2-21_ Writing Piece: _"My Favorite Day"_

	scaffolded
Questions I have:	☐ How do my ideas flow? ☐ What do you notice about the way my writing is organized? ☐ Where could I add more details? ☐ What areas could be improved? ☐ _what do you think about the dialogue in my story?_ ☐ _____
Feedback:	_The story has some events that seem out of place. It jumps around too quickly._ _The dialogue sounds good, but you could add more description about how the teacher talks does she sound worried or happy?_

What I'm doing with this feedback:

I am going to move some of my story events and add some transition words so that the order makes more sense. I will also add some descriptive details to show that the teacher is feeling excited when she talks.

©2019 Simplify Writing® Updated 2022   3

Scaffold, If Needed

For students who struggle to come up with questions, you can scaffold using a form with pre-populated questions. Use this sparingly, as you want students to ask real questions they have and not just check a box. Try to move your students toward the blank form after using this a few times. The blank form can be found in both the Appendix and downloadable files.

You can incorporate a lesson on how to give and receive peer feedback in just one day using this simple peer feedback lesson. It's a great way to introduce the concept and get students thinking about what quality feedback looks like. Even though this is a single-day lesson, you should refer back to the organizers from this lesson many times throughout the year in order to continue to practice and refine your peer feedback practices.

Once you finish the lesson, students can then directly practice it during their independent writing time. This is a good time to walk around and help them focus their questions and feedback better. Dedicate the entire block to practicing feedback, so you can be confident that students really understand the process from start to finish.

Although it may be simpler to give feedback ourselves, structuring time for peer feedback allows for more opportunities for students to learn and grow as writers. By giving students the opportunity to provide feedback to their peers, we are not only increasing student engagement and motivation, but also improving the quality of their work. It allows writers to get a different perspective on their writing and identify areas that need improvement. With pre-planning and a lot of modeling, incorporating peer feedback into our classrooms can have a positive impact on our students' writing.

PEER FEEDBACK FAQs

HOW OFTEN SHOULD I USE PEER FEEDBACK?

Use it as often as possible! At first, build it into your units so that students get practice. Then, let them try it themselves at your peer feedback station while you're working on small group or conferring with students.

WHEN SHOULD I FIRST USE IT?

You can start teaching your students about peer feedback in your units as early as you'd like. For independent peer feedback opportunities like the station, wait until your procedures are solidly in place before beginning. You want your students to practice just writing independently for a while before you add anything to your block.

WHERE IN THE WRITING PROCESS DOES IT BEST FIT?

Peer feedback is great at any step in the writing process. Students should be getting feedback often, and not just waiting until they've finished a rough draft.

WHAT IF MY STUDENTS GIVE TERRIBLE FEEDBACK?

If you teach about peer feedback and model it, your students have a greater chance for success with it when they start on their own. The more they practice it with your support, the better they'll get at it.

WHAT IF STUDENTS GO TO THE PEER FEEDBACK STATION JUST TO HANG OUT WITH THEIR FRIENDS?

It's inevitable that when a student sees a friend head back to the station, they'll be tempted to follow. Don't let concerns about this stop you from including necessary collaboration activities like peer feedback in your classroom. Make it clear to your students that you want them to get feedback from different people. If you notice a pattern for certain students, pull them aside and talk to them. If you continue to have issues with certain students after talking to them, take away their access to the station for a week and then try again.

HOW SHOULD I PAIR STUDENTS?

There's no right or wrong way to pair students when you're doing an organized peer feedback opportunity. Every student, no matter what level they're at, can give feedback when their partner reads a part of their writing and asks them specific questions.

HOW LONG SHOULD PEER FEEDBACK TAKE?

Peer feedback should take less than 15 minutes, but 10 minutes is preferable (5 min./person). It really depends on how many questions their peers have. Sometimes students just have one quick question they need answered for their writing. Other times, they'll have a lot of questions, or there will be a lot of discussion back and forth. Guide students toward getting just one or two small pieces of feedback and then revising their writing so that they don't get overwhelmed by a very long feedback session.

HOW DO I GET THEM TO FOCUS ON CONTENT RELATED FEEDBACK RATHER THAN OBVIOUS SPELLING/CONVENTION ERRORS?

This is all about teaching them to ask focused questions about their writing and give specific feedback to their peers. The more you model that and show them how to use the peer feedback form in the context of their conference, the better they will get at focusing on the content.

HOW CAN I ENGAGE STUDENTS WHO ARE RELUCTANT TO SHARE THEIR WRITING WITH A PEER?

Making this a fun, and safe, experience is so important for these students. This is yet another reason why we practice giving meaningful feedback as a class before having them do it on their own. They'll see what it looks like with the class, then be more comfortable when they're participating themselves.

WHAT DO STUDENTS DO WHILE THEY'RE WAITING AT THE PEER FEEDBACK STATION?

When a student gets back to the station, they need to fill out a peer feedback form. If they're waiting a while for another student, they should continue to work on their writing as much as possible.

WHAT IF THE PEER FEEDBACK STATION HAS TOO MANY STUDENTS?

The number of students will grow toward the end of the writing block when more students are finished. I recommend having students meet at their desks if it gets too crowded. There shouldn't be more than a few students back there in the first 10 minutes.

WHAT IF MY STUDENTS GO STRAIGHT TO THE PEER FEEDBACK STATION INSTEAD OF TRYING TO WRITE?

If this starts to become a problem, set a 10-minute timer before students can utilize the station area. Tell them that they must have tried something in their writing before coming back to fill out the peer feedback form.

Reflect and Plan

Reflect on what you envision peer feedback will look like in your classroom. Determine when you will give your students the peer feedback lesson. From there, decide when and where your students can practice it with your support over the next unit. Prepare your peer feedback center for when you're ready to use it

CHAPTER 15

Support Students with Learning Disabilities

Providing adequate support to students with learning disabilities can be a challenging task, but it's one of the most important and rewarding things we can do. From the 2009–2010 to the 2020–2021 school year, the number of students who received special education services under the Individuals with Disabilities Education Act (IDEA) increased from 6.5 million, or 13% of total public school enrollment, to 7.2 million, or 15% of total public school enrollment (National Center for Education Statistics, 2021). Despite this growth, many teacher preparation programs don't provide strategies to support these students during writing instruction. In this chapter, we explore various strategies that you can use to successfully create an accommodating classroom environment for your writers with learning disabilities.

HOW LEARNING DISABILITIES AFFECT WRITING ABILITY

Students with learning disabilities often have difficulty with language and communication, which can make writing a particularly challenging task. For example, students with dyslexia may struggle with reading and spelling, while students with dysgraphia may have difficulty with handwriting and fine motor skills. By taking these difficulties into account, you can provide targeted instruction and accommodations that can help these students overcome their challenges and become more confident and effective writers.

Students with learning disabilities often have unique strengths and talents that can be overlooked or underutilized in a traditional writing curriculum. For example, a student with dyslexia may have a strong visual imagination and excel at creating illustrations or graphic designs, while a student with dysgraphia may have a good ear for rhythm and meter and excel at poetry. By providing opportunities for students to explore and develop their strengths, teachers can help them find their own voices as writers and build their self-esteem.

You can create a more inclusive and equitable learning environment for all students by providing inclusive instruction and accommodations for students with learning disabilities. This may include providing multiple formats for written assignments, such as audio recordings or dictation software, as well as using different teaching strategies, such as hands-on or visual aids, to ensure that all students can succeed during your lessons.

The great news is that a lot of the strategies you've already put in place will help support your students with learning disabilities.

The following strategies for students with learning disabilities are already included with the approaches in this book:

1. Provide clear procedures.
2. Model a skill using a clear graphic organizer.
3. Create a personalized learning plan for each student.
4. Encourage students to set small goals and celebrate their accomplishments.
5. Modify teaching methods to better meet the needs of each student.
6. Be patient and supportive – remember that every student learns differently.

There are several different types of learning disabilities that can affect a person's ability to learn and process information. The following is a list of common learning disabilities and some of the strategies you can try with these students. Some of these strategies, such as assistive technology and pencil grips, can be used with individual students, while others can be added to your general writing block.

Strategies for Common Learning Disabilities that Affect Writers		
Learning Disability	Description	Strategies
Dyslexia	A learning disability that affects a person's ability to read and interpret words and letters.	• Use pictures and simple graphic organizers. • Explicitly teach spelling and grammar rules instead of just correcting errors. • Use assistive technology like text-to-speech and word-processing editing tools.
Dysgraphia	A learning disability that affects a person's ability to write legibly and produce written work.	• Provide pencil grips. • Use paper with color-coded lines for letter placement. • Provide a copy of the teacher model.
ADHD	Attention deficit hyperactivity disorder, which can affect a person's ability to focus, pay attention, and control their impulses.	• Encourage active engagement during lessons. • Make sure you have consistent and predictable routines. • Use visual aids.
Auditory processing disorder	A learning disability that affects a person's ability to process and interpret auditory information, such as spoken words.	• Give short, simple written directions. • Use order words like *first*, *next*, *last*. • Do not ask to listen and write at the same time. • Check for understanding.
Visual processing disorder	A learning disability that affects a person's ability to process and interpret visual information, such as written words and images.	• Give verbal directions. • Use tools (like text-to-speech) to read teacher models and other text aloud to them. • Reduce visual distractions and keep organizers simple.
Nonverbal learning disability	A learning disability that affects a person's ability to interpret and use nonverbal cues, such as facial expressions and body language.	• Identify a nonverbal signal for if they need a social break. • Scaffold discussion and peer work until they are comfortable. • Give a quiet place to work.

This isn't an exhaustive list of all of the learning disabilities you'll see in your classroom. It's also important to note that even students with the same learning disability can have different challenges. Our goal is to arm these students with the skills and resources they need to succeed while also providing encouragement and fostering an environment of inclusion. Trying one or more of these strategies to see if they help your students is a great place to start.

Make sure to review the IEPs for individual student accommodations. This will prepare you to make any accommodations necessary during your writing block, but they can also give you insight into what strategies work well for these students. When you combine these strategies with what you're already doing to help them fill in learning gaps, you should begin to see measurable growth from these students.

Student Tracking

Student*	Learning Disability	Modifications or Accommodations	Strategies to Try	Progress Notes

*Use student initials for privacy.

This page must be kept private and for your planning use only. It should be secured in the same way as copies of student IEPs

D15.1 Strategy Tracker for Students with Learning Disabilities

While it can be challenging to provide adequate support to students with learning disabilities, it is essential. Use the strategies in this chapter, along with each student's individual learning goals, to successfully create an accommodating classroom environment. By providing the proper support during the writing block, you will give your students the best chance to succeed.

SUPPORTING STUDENTS WITH LEARNING DISABILITIES FAQs

WHAT DO YOU DO WITH STUDENTS WHO GET PULLED OUT DURING WRITING FOR SPECIAL EDUCATION SERVICES?

If you have students who are pulled out during writing time, connect with their resource teacher to see how you can work together to support them. Stay in communication so that you know where they are with their goals and can support them during the times they are in your class.

SHOULD I MODIFY THE AMOUNT OF WRITING THESE STUDENTS ARE EXPECTED TO PRODUCE?

It depends on each student's learning disability and their individual ability level. Some of your students may be able to produce the same amount of text as other students, but they need extra support with spelling and handwriting.

SHOULD I ALLOW VOICE-TO-TEXT OR OTHER TYPES OF ADAPTIVE TOOLS?

Absolutely! Any tool that helps support the student should be encouraged. Teaching them to use these tools will be helpful not only in school, but in their future careers.

WHEN DO I EMPHASIZE/PRACTICE HANDWRITING?

For the students who need handwriting practice, you can introduce tools and strategies in small group. Then, continue to have students apply these in their own writing. There's nothing wrong with assigning them extra handwriting practice whenever they have time to work on it. Just make sure that they have enough time during their independent writing block to apply this practice in their writing pieces.

SHOULD I STILL USE ON-GRADE-LEVEL MATERIALS AND PROMPTS WITH THESE STUDENTS?

Yes! Your students with learning disabilities should still be a part of your whole group mini-lesson and work on what the rest of the class is working on. You will modify expectations or provide tools to support them with their individual needs during their independent writing time.

SHOULD I ASSESS WITH GRADE-LEVEL STANDARDS/EXPECTATIONS?

Please see the grading chapter for more information on mastery-based grading and how to use rubrics with students who are below grade level.

Reflect and Plan

Review any IEPs for students in your class with learning disabilities. Create a list of their accommodations and additional strategies you can try with each of them. Don't overcomplicate it by trying too many strategies at once. Aim to start with one individual strategy at a time and see what larger strategies you can build into your writing block.

CHAPTER 16

Support English Language Learners

Like our native English speakers, our English Language Learners (ELLs) have their own unique needs and challenges to overcome. Many of the students have learned the foundation for writing instruction in their native language, while some may be completely new to writing. Every student is at a different place in their English acquisition journey. This means they will have different learning gaps and proficiency levels.

Although our ELLs have many obstacles to overcome when juggling learning a new language while learning academic content at the same time, we should avoid approaching our work with them from a deficit perspective (Fenner and Snyder, 2017). The great thing is that you're already providing a student-centered environment during your writing block. This is the best way to focus both the assets your ELLs have and their individual learning needs (Fenner and Snyder, 2017).

The English language has many complex words and rules of grammar. For example, verb tenses, plurals, sentence structure, and punctuation can all be confusing to students who are not familiar with them. Along with the language gap as they're continuing to develop their English Language Proficiency, ELLs may have difficulty understanding the nuances of certain words or expressions and how they are used in different contexts. Additionally, the cultural context of a student's native language may not match that of English, so they may have difficulty using certain expressions or metaphors used in English writing. Small group is a great opportunity to provide them with targeted grammar instruction to grow their understanding of these concepts.

Another way you can support your ELLs is by providing direct vocabulary instruction. These students need direct instruction in vocabulary to help them build a more meaningful understanding of words and how they are used in writing. Vocabulary instruction can be tailored to the needs of small groups of students who are at similar levels of language proficiency and should focus on using words correctly in context. This can include activities such as working with synonyms, antonyms, homophones, and word families; playing word games or reading activities that encourage students to use new words; and reviewing grammar rules related to usage within sentences.

Frontloading vocabulary is an effective strategy for ELL students because it provides them with a foundation of words and definitions they can reference when writing. This gives them the necessary tools to accurately express themselves in their written work, which increases their confidence in using English. Additionally, by having familiarity with the words beforehand, ELLs can focus on other aspects of writing, such as organization and style, rather than trying to remember word meaning or grammar rules.

Focusing on vocabulary is beneficial for all learners, not just your ELLs. In addition to providing vocabulary tools to students who need them, you can front-load content vocabulary into your whole group writing lessons. You can also use your teacher model to review commonly confused words. Teaching in a border town in Arizona led me to naturally include more vocabulary activities in my writing block, and it turned out to improve student writing overall.

My favorite tools to support ELLs are simple, yet effective. Sentence and paragraph frames provide a structure for students to organize their thoughts and ideas, allowing them to express themselves more confidently. Graphic organizers also help students to categorize and make connections between new vocabulary and concepts. These tools help to break down complex language and make it more accessible for ELL students, providing a foundation for them to build upon as they continue to develop their language skills. The tools and templates that are mentioned in this chapter are available in the downloadable resources under file D16.1.

⊘ File D16.1 Resources for English Language Learners

SENTENCE FRAMES

Many of your emerging and developing ELLs may be focusing on writing full sentences in English. Sentence frames are the best way to help these students understand the structure of the sentence, including rules on capitalization and punctuation. You can customize sentence frames for your writing unit's topic and genre to help these students form sentences like their peers. This allows you to modify the expectations for individual students, while still using the same whole group lesson.

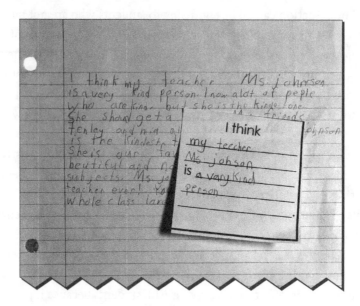

Printing sentence frames on sticky notes is a great way to help your ELLs write an individual sentence. In this example, the teacher has provided extra support for the topic sentence. You can also use the same idea for paragraph writing by creating a paragraph frame with the entire structure of the paragraph created with fill-in-the blank areas for them to write in. This can easily be created in a word document with size 16–18 font.

My favorite book is _____. It was

written by _____. I like this story

because_____.

My favorite part of the book is when _____

_____.

You should definitely read _____!

VOCABULARY TOOLS

For English Language Learners, graphic organizers are particularly useful in supporting both their language development and comprehension. By actively engaging with the information through visual representation, they can make connections and build deeper understanding. Using graphic organizers for vocabulary can help ELLs develop their language skills and use new words in the correct context.

There are many vocabulary tools you can use to support your ELLs during the writing block. It's important to choose one that works with your students and be consistent with it. A simple graphic organizer is all you need to pre-teach content vocabulary or help students create a glossary of new words. The organizer pictured shows how two content vocabulary words for an informational writing piece on a scientific topic can be defined and visually represented. This can be used with your whole class to help them use content vocabulary in their writing, or it can be used with individual students for basic vocabulary.

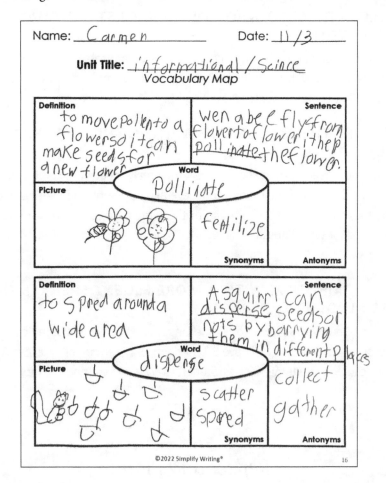

Another useful tool is a word wall, where vocabulary words are displayed in the classroom and regularly referred to by the teacher and students. This provides students with a visual reference for new words and helps to reinforce their understanding. You can also have students create a word glossary with the words they most often confuse.

Properly supporting our ELLs during writing instruction is important for many reasons. We know that they come to us with different academic backgrounds and levels of proficiency in both their native language as well as in English. By approaching our work with them from a culturally responsive standpoint, we can better serve the needs of all our students.

SUPPORTING ELLs FAQs

SHOULD I TRANSLATE THE MENTOR TEXT AND/OR WORKSHEETS INTO THEIR FIRST LANGUAGE?

Research says that using their native language supports their acquisition of English, so you may translate anything they need to read if it helps support their understanding. New AI tools are making translations increasingly accurate, so find one online that's quick and easy to use. Translating an entire piece is more commonly used with the very beginning ELLs, but you may find a tool that allows for your students to translate on demand is useful for your intermediate ELLs.

SHOULD I ALLOW THEM TO WRITE IN THEIR FIRST LANGUAGE AND THEN TRANSLATE TO ENGLISH?

All forms of writing are encouraged! If your student is more comfortable doing this, then find ways to support them. You can work with them in small group using sentence frames to help them become more proficient at writing complete sentences in English.

SHOULD I MODIFY THE AMOUNT OF WRITING THEY ARE EXPECTED TO PRODUCE?

Don't automatically modify any expectations unless they really need it. Like all your learners, these modifications are individualized. If they can output several paragraphs and need assistance with spelling and grammar, they should keep their writing at the same pace as the rest of your class. Alternatively, if they can't speak or write English at all, their goals will be around basic vocabulary and forming simple sentences to start.

IS IT BETTER TO PAIR THEM WITH A MORE FLUENT SPEAKER OR WITH ANOTHER ELL STUDENT?

If you have another student who speaks their home language, it can be encouraging for them to work together. This is especially true when you have ELL students of different ability levels. A student who is close to proficiency can be a great mentor to a student who is just starting their journey.

Reflect and Plan

Reflect on what support systems you already have in place to support your students. How can these also help your ELLs? Can you modify or add anything to your lessons to support these students? If you don't have any ELLs right now, write about what you learned from the chapter that you may use in the future if any join your class.

CHAPTER 17

Grade with a Student-Centered Approach

There are countless approaches to grading your students' work, and you don't always have complete control over them. You can, however, make small tweaks to how you input grades to better track each student's individual growth. More teachers are taking on some form of student-centered grading, as it stresses growth over letter grades and has been known to foster stronger relationships between educators and their students. In this chapter, we look at what a student-centered approach to grading entails in two different grading systems: mastery-based grading and standards-based grading.

MASTERY-BASED GRADING

Let's say you have a student named Carmen, who moved to the United States from Mexico two years ago. You've been using sentence frames and other supports with her, and she's grown a lot during the writing block. You grade the final draft of her writing piece with the rest of the pile, using the on-grade-level rubric. You're excited to see that she's scoring a lot more "2s" than "1s" now. It's an exciting amount of growth for her personally, but she technically is still "failing."

Rubrics have value when grading the final draft of a writing piece because you've had a chance to support your writers with small group, peer, and adult feedback. They provide a good overall look at where the student falls with the grade-level standards. The question remains: How do you ensure that Carmen's goals and progress also make it into the grade book? The answer is mastery-based grading, and it can be combined with most traditional grading systems.

With mastery-based grading, you only enter skills into the grade book when a student has mastered them. They get full credit for mastering the skill (100%). One week, you may have a student who is working on writing three complete body sentences, while other students in your class have mastered an on-grade-level skill from your mini-lesson. This requires a lot of extra skill-based entries in your grade book, but it also allows for students to see their progress and growth reflected in their grades. This is integral to building students' sense of self-worth in the classroom (Farah, 2021). I recommend you use a mix of grading their final drafts using your on-grade-level rubric **and** mastery-based grading.

Use Correct Punctuation	Write an introduction sentence	Write 3 body sentences	Write a conclusion sentence	Narrative Final Draft (Grade-Level Rubric)
10/10	10/10	10/10	10/10	70% (10)

A mastery-based grading system requires a major change in the way we think about grades. Many teachers are concerned about what will happen if a student who is behind grade level comes out with a grade equal to a student on grade level. We need to take the competition between students over grades out of the equation and focus on individual student development (Zerwin, 2020). In our traditional grading systems, there are many instances where a higher grade doesn't equal more effort from the student.

For your students who lack motivation because they can't see any way to catch up to their classmates, it's very motivating as they start to see positive marks in the gradebook as they master things at their own pace. There's no evidence that supports lower grades motivating students to do better (Feldman, 2018). It also allows for everyone involved in the students' education to see their personal progress, while still seeing where they're at compared to on-grade-level standards.

The most common issue with this system is that some students won't master something every week, but the school requires a weekly grade for each subject. Sadly, when schools require a certain number of grades each week, it takes the focus off our students and puts added stress on teachers. You can still use mastery-based grading by inputting the skill they're working on and giving them a progress grade. For example, if they're working on building sentences in small group and are close to mastery, you can input a 7/10 for that skill. It isn't a perfect solution, but it can help meet the grading requirements you have to follow.

Before you get overwhelmed thinking about having to put in different grade entries for each student, remember that many of your students will still be working toward the same goals. Your students who are on or above grade level will work on the goals related to your whole group mini-lesson. Your other students are likely grouped together with certain skills that pertain to this writing type, especially if you're using small groups with shared goals. Small group is where I get most of my gradebook entries for the students who aren't working on grade level.

STANDARDS-BASED GRADING

Many schools have adopted a standards-based grading system, which is an improvement from most tradition grading systems. In standards-based grading, student proficiency is measured using well-defined objectives, usually related to the grade-level standards (Tomlinson & McTighe, 2006). In most standards-based systems, an overall grade is entered for each standard. This grade is usually obtained by some sort of end-of-unit assessment, which is usually the final draft of a writing piece.

If your school uses standards-based grading with only a single grade for each standard, I encourage you to take an average of all the work the student has done to work toward mastery of the standard, no matter what level it's conducted at. Also, make sure to make a note of their progress with below-grade-level skills in the comments for students and their families to see. Most schools who use this grading system still allow teachers to input multiple entries into the gradebook and an average is taken. This means that you can give students multiple opportunities to work on elements of the grade-level standards and improve their overall grade.

For students like Carmen, the supports you have built into your writing block can help her work toward a higher grade for the standards that every student in your class are graded on. Although it may not be an on-grade-level skill, you can input grades for small group activities like mastering sentences toward the overall score for a standard because it's a building block element of the standard. That's just one example, but any activity where they show mastery (or working toward mastery) can be input into your grade book to show their progress.

What to Grade	What Not to Grade
• Small group work	• Rough drafts
• Grammar activities that are scaffolded	• Homework
• Final draft of writing pieces	• Journaling
• Writing in other subject areas	
• Other written tasks that students have had support with	

GRADING TOOLS

Two useful tools for grading the final draft of student writing pieces are exemplars and rubrics. Together, these apparatuses help to set clear guidelines, which helps make sure that grading is equitable. They also help you have a clear idea of what you're looking for in students' final drafts in order to score them.

Exemplars are model pieces of writing that serve as a standard for a particular assignment or task. You can use exemplars in grading writing by comparing students' work to the exemplars to determine how closely the students' writing aligns with the expectations set by the rubric. Exemplars can also be used to give students concrete examples of what good writing looks like, which can help them understand the expectations and improve their own writing skills. You can view four sample exemplars in the Appendix of this book.

One of my favorite lessons to use with my students is highlighting key elements from the rubric in exemplars of different levels. Not only does this show them what is expected to be in their writing, it helps them see how their writing is scored. This lesson can be done at any time in the writing process, but most teachers use it toward the end of the rough draft.

Although rubrics usually follow on-grade-level standards, it's fair to use them to grade an end product like a final draft because students have received support during the writing process through small group and feedback opportunities. Your students will both work on on-grade-level skills and fill in individual learning gaps with your support. This will be reflected in their final drafts, and that hard work should receive a fair grade. Not only do rubrics make grading more efficient and objective by providing clear criteria and descriptions, but they can also be used to set expectations during the writing process.

Using a student-friendly rubric has numerous benefits for both you and your students. First, it provides clear and specific expectations for the assignment, allowing students to understand what is expected of them and how their work will be evaluated. This helps them focus on the important aspects of the assignment and improve their performance. Second, it empowers your students to take ownership of their learning by allowing them to self-assess and reflect on their work, which enhances their understanding and mastery of the overall writing process. If you're looking to use self-assessment for your grade book, this is a simple way to do it.

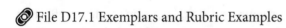 File D17.1 Exemplars and Rubric Examples

SCORING WITH RUBRICS

The question remains, how do you translate a rubric score into a fair grade? With the complicated nature of a rubric, it can seem overwhelming to calculate or result in scores that don't reflect the hard work your students have put into their drafts. This is especially an issue with our students who are working toward goals that are behind grade level.

While using a rubric to score writing is common practice, it can be challenging to translate these rubric scores into a number for the grade book. Traditionally, a student who receives all 4s, or 20 points, on the rubric earns a grade of 100%, while a student who receives all 2s, or 10 points, on the rubric earns a grade of 50%. However, this method of grading makes it very difficult for some writers to ever receive a passing grade.

Instead, I recommend using a more equitable method of grading. The following chart uses a shifted scale that eliminates scores below 55%, allowing students to earn credit for their effort, and maximizing a student's potential writing score. My rubrics are divided into five categories: Focus, Organization, Elaboration, Language & Vocabulary, and Conventions. Students receive a score for each category at one of four levels of writing: Advanced, Proficient, Basic, and Below Basic. So, the maximum score for a piece of writing is 20 points, while the lowest score a student may receive is 5 points. After scoring a writing piece for each category on the rubric, add the points for each category and find the total on the chart to determine the final grade.

Writing Rubric Scoring Guide			
Rubric Score	**Percentage**	**Rubric Score**	**Percentage**
20	100%	12	76%
19	97%	11	73%
18	94%	10	70%
17	91%	9	67%
16	88%	8	64%
15	85%	7	61%
14	82%	6	58%
13	79%	5	55%

The Appendix includes a Rubric Scoring Guide along with several Sample Scoring examples. These are also available for download.

File D17.2 Rubric Scoring Guide

Rubrics and exemplars are two powerful tools that can help you grade student writing effectively and equitably. By using these resources, you can be sure that you're looking for the right things in their final drafts and score them accordingly. As you begin planning for your next unit, take some time to reflect on how you'll use rubrics and exemplars to make grading a simpler and more transparent process. How will the supports you put in place be reflected in their writing when it's time to grade it? Having a plan for how you'll use these resources will help ensure that your grading is as fair and effective as possible.

GRADING FAQs

WHAT IF STUDENTS DON'T EVEN TRY?

I like to say that I make it impossible for my students to not do anything. It's our job to support them in a way that helps get them past roadblocks and gain confidence in writing. If they struggle to write independently, they're at least working with me in small group to produce something. That being said, there are going to be some students who don't put their full effort in, and that will be reflected in their grade with both mastery-based grading and standards-based grading.

HOW DO I TRANSLATE SCORES ON THE RUBRIC TO A NUMBER OR PERCENTAGE GRADE IF MY RUBRIC HAS A DIFFERENT TOTAL SCORE?

Although many rubrics follow a similar scoring system, there may be some that have a different number of categories or total points. That's okay! Make your own table using my example that matches the total score of your rubric, ensuring that you're eliminating scores below 55%.

SHOULD I SHARE MY SCORING GUIDE WITH THE RUBRIC?

Yes, you should attach your scoring guide and rubric for both your use and transparency with your students!

SHOULD I GRADE EVERY WRITING PIECE?

I truly believe that every final draft deserves a score. If you've taken the time to teach the writing process step-by-step, and your students have had ample opportunity to get feedback, a lot of work has gone into this. Quick writes that don't provide opportunity for feedback and revision should not be graded.

WHAT IF MY SCHOOL TELLS US WE CAN'T GRADE WRITING THAT A STUDENT HAS HAD ANY HELP WITH?

Writing is a process that requires feedback and support throughout. If adult authors are encouraged to do research, get feedback, and go through multiple edits before their pieces are judged, we should offer our students the same opportunity. I would strongly disagree with this policy.

SHOULD I ASSIGN A NEW PROMPT OF THE SAME GENRE FOR STUDENTS TO COMPLETE IN ONE DAY FOR THE FINAL GRADE TO ASSESS WHAT THEY'VE LEARNED?

No, a rushed writing piece should not be used as their overall grade for a standard or a large part of their grade. Even if students have help and support throughout the writing process, their final draft reflects what they've learned and worked toward as an individual. Grade the writing pieces they put work into, not something they were rushed through without ample time or support.

Reflect and Plan

Download the grading tools and keep them in a place where it's easy for you to access when it's time for you to grade their writing pieces. Reflect on how the practices in this chapter can help you provide meaningful and fair grades for all of your students.

LETTER HOME: WRITING SUPPORT

Dear Parent/Guardian,

This year our class is making writing a priority. We want to help students become strong writers by giving them time to write every day, in all subject areas. We'll have daily writing lessons to directly model the writing skills we want our students to master. Our goal is to make writing meaningful and exciting by empowering students to share their opinions and ideas.

How Can You Help?

Writing is a real-world task. There are many opportunities to incorporate authentic writing practice at home, such as:

- Write letters or emails to a family member.
- Keep a journal while on vacation to record and reflect on your experiences.
- Write an online review for a book you've read or a movie you've seen.
- Rewrite the ending to your favorite book.
- Make up a silly song or poem.
- Research your family history and write a narrative about what you learn.
- Send a persuasive letter to your local newspaper to inspire change in the community.
- Use interesting photos or images to spark an imaginative story.
- Create an instruction manual for a friend or neighbor.

Tips for Making It Meaningful:

Provide a place for writing and keep it stocked with fun materials such as decorative notebooks, blank paper, pencils, crayons, etc.

Model writing for your students. Point out the various ways writing is used to communicate with others and let your children see you as writer.

Allow students to experiment and have fun with their writing. Emphasize the process rather than perfection and praise your students' efforts.

Find ways for students to share their writing with family and friends in authentic ways. Record students reading their writing aloud, create and illustrate a book, or use an online app to publish writing digitally.

I appreciate your support in making writing a priority this year.

Sincerely,

PRE-ASSESSMENT SPREADSHEET EXAMPLE: WHOLE GROUP (FILE A1)

Interest & Stamina	Sentence Writing	Paragraph Writing	Complexity of Ideas	Technology Knowledge	Other: Elements of Narrative	Other: Informational Structure	Other:
What this means for my whole group instruction:	What this means for my whole group instruction:	What this means for my whole group instruction:	What this means for my whole group instruction:	What this means for my whole group instruction:	What this means for my whole group instruction:	What this means for my whole group instruction:	What this means for my whole group instruction:

PRE-ASSESSMENT SPREADSHEET EXAMPLE: GRAMMAR KNOCKOUT LIST (FILE A2)

Grammar Skill	When will this unit be taught?	Date Completed	Notes:
List the grammar skills you need to cover from greatest impact to least impact and add notes as you cover each skill.			

PRE-ASSESSMENT SPREADSHEET EXAMPLE: INDIVIDUAL STRUGGLES (FILE A3)

Student Names	Stamina	Sentence Writing	Paragraph Writing	Complexity of Ideas	Grammar & Spelling (Highest Priority)	Other
Enter student names and mark categories where the student struggles with an X. List specific grammar skills in that column.						

PRE-ASSESSMENT SPREADSHEET EXAMPLE: STUDENT GOALS (FILE A4)

Student Names	Focus Skill	Progress Notes	Date Mastered

File D5.1 Pre-Assessment Spreadsheet Sample

Famous Authors Who Didn't Give Up

A Passage about Struggling Writers

By Rachel Peachey

It's hard to imagine any publisher rejecting famous books like *Dune* or *Harry Potter*. These books are classics, beloved by many people around the world. Yet, the authors of these books and many others struggled to get published. Their amazing stories show just how determined authors need to be to succeed.

Dune, by Frank Herbert, is a famous science-fiction novel that has now been made into a movie. However, Herbert received rejection letters from 23 different publishers. Even after all that, Herbert's novel was accepted by Chilton Books. This publisher usually published car manuals. Despite all that, *Dune* eventually grew popular and even won important awards! Today, it remains the best-selling science fiction novel of all time.

Similarly, J.K. Rowling's first Harry Potter book was rejected twelve times. When she found a publisher for the book, the editor wasn't enthusiastic. He wasn't convinced the book would achieve much success. Today, the series has broken many world records. *The Deathly Hallows* earned the title of most books printed in the first printing with 12 million copies. Despite this great success, J.K. Rowling has still experienced rejection. Using a pen name, she sent off a mystery novel to various publishers who rejected it. Finally, *The Cuckoo's Calling* was published, becoming a series of its own!

The famous novel *Little Women* also got a rough start. In one of her rejection letters, Louisa May Alcott was reportedly told to "Stick to teaching…you can't write." Thankfully, Alcott didn't give up and found a publisher for the book. First published in 1868, *Little Women* is still a popular novel today that has even been made into a movie. Alcott also went on to write many more books, including a few sequels to *Little Women*.

Yet another author who experienced rejection is Agatha Christie. Today, she is known for her 65 detective novels and 14 short-story collections. Christie is easily one of the world's most famous mystery writers. Yet, her first novel was never even published. However, in one rejection letter, the agent suggested that Christie try writing another novel. After more rejections, the novel was finally published, giving her the start she needed as an author. Christie's books are so popular they've been translated into over 100 languages.

Despite many rejections and difficulties along the way, great authors don't give up. Thanks to their persistence and determination, we can now enjoy reading their books today! These famous authors also set an important example for hopeful writers. With their example, they teach upcoming writers to keep working toward their goals even when things are tough.

SMALL GROUP PLANNING PAGES: SKILL PLANNER

Monday	Tuesday	Wednesday

Thursday	Friday	*Notes*

SMALL GROUP PLANNING PAGES: DAILY ORGANIZER

Date:

Lesson Objective(s):

Student Names:

Lesson Information:

Materials:

Session Notes:

SMALL GROUP PLANNING PAGES: STUDENT GOAL PAGE

Name:

My goal:

Today I learned: _____
_____
_____
_____
_____
_____
_____
_____
_____
_____.

I will use this in my writing by: _____
_____
_____
_____
_____
_____
_____
_____
_____.

Tools I will use to meet my goal:

SMALL GROUP PLANNING PAGES: SKILLS I'M WORKING ON

Name:	

Skill:	**How to Practice This in My Writing:**
Date Mastered:	
Date Mastered:	
Date Mastered:	

PRE-CONFERENCE FORM

Name: _____ Date: _____

Something going well in my writing is:	
Something that's challenging or I'm unsure of in my writing is:	
Two specific questions I have: 1. 2.	
Feedback I received:	
Next Step:	

COMMON STUDENT GOALS & STRATEGIES FOR INFORMATIONAL/ OPINION WRITING

	Goal	Strategy
Focus	Introduce the topic in a way that engages the reader	"Write three different hooks and ask a partner for feedback on choosing the best one."
	Use a clear thesis statement to provide a focus for the writing	"Reread the prompt. Cross out the question words (who, what, where, etc.) from the prompt and turn the prompt into a statement. Answer the question using your main idea."
	Keep the focus of the writing consistent throughout	"Underline your thesis statement. Read each detail sentence from your body paragraph. Cross off the details that don't directly support your thesis."
	Tie the writing together with a focused conclusion	"Write a sentence that restates your thesis statement and main ideas. Reword it in three different ways and ask a partner for feedback."
Organization	Group related information together in paragraphs or sections	"Highlight each of the categories on your planning page in a different color. Then, highlight the details that match each category in the same color."
	Link ideas using transition words	"Use the transitions bookmark to add a transition to the beginning of each paragraph."
	Include useful text features	"Reread each body paragraph. Add headings that tell readers the main idea of that paragraph. Read your headings to a partner to see if they can predict what will be in each paragraph."
Elaboration: Key Details	Use several different types of information to develop the topic	"Highlight the quotes in your body paragraph with one color. Use another color for the paraphrased facts, and a different color for definitions or descriptions. Make sure each paragraph includes at least one of each color."
	Connect all elaborations to the main idea	"Explain why the evidence is important using an elaboration sentence stem."
Language & Vocabulary	Use precise language and vocabulary to explain the topic	"Circle at least three nouns in your text. Verbally define each noun to a partner. If you can't define the word, use a thesaurus to replace it with a stronger, more specific word. Repeat this with adjectives and verbs, if needed."
Conventions	Use correct punctuation	"Check the end of each sentence for the correct end mark and circle it."
	Follow capitalization rules	"Highlight proper nouns, titles, and the first letter in each sentence to check for capital letters."
	Vary sentences using proper grammar	"Label the sentences in your body paragraph as simple, compound, or complex. Use your notes page to help you. Include at least one of each type in every paragraph."
	Use correct spelling	"Meet with a partner to help you circle any misspelled words. Use a dictionary to fix them."

COMMON STUDENT GOALS & STRATEGIES FOR NARRATIVE WRITING

	Goal	Strategy
Focus	Engage the reader	"Write three different beginnings for your story. Include dialogue, action, and/or sensory details. Then, ask a partner for feedback on choosing the best one."
	Establish a situation, setting, and important characters	"Reread your exposition. Highlight each detail that tells about the characters, setting, or situation. Add a piece of action that shows the character's problem instead of telling about it. Use the five senses to describe the setting."
	Use a consistent point of view throughout	"Underline all the pronouns in the narration. Check to make sure they are all either first-person (I, me, my) or third-person (s/he, they)."
Organization	Use a clear sequence of events	"Plot your story events on a plot diagram and reread it to make sure the events flow in order."
	Shift between story events using transition words	"Use the transitions bookmark to add a transition each time something new happens in the story."
Elaboration: Key Details	Include relevant dialogue	"Use the dialogue bookmark to add dialogue that shows a character's thoughts/feelings."
	Create authentic characters	"Make a list of the character's internal and external traits. Add these details to your story."
	Describe the setting with specific details	"Underline details in each paragraph that show when or where that part of the story takes place."
	Fully develop the conflict and resolution	"Put a star next to each story event that tells about the main conflict in the story. Build tension by adding two more details that make the problem larger."
Language & Vocabulary	Use sensory and/or figurative language to create rich descriptions	"Make a sensory chart with details that tell how things look, sound, smell, taste, and feel. Add these details to your story."
	Use specific words or phrases to create a certain mood	"Think about the mood you want to create. Make a list of feeling words that show the character's emotions and relate to that mood. Add these to your story."
Conventions	Use correct punctuation	"Check the end of each sentence for the correct end mark and circle it."
	Follow capitalization rules	"Highlight proper nouns, titles, and the first letter in each sentence to check for capital letters."
	Vary sentences using proper grammar	"Label the sentences in your body paragraph as simple, compound, or complex. Use your notes page to help you. Include at least one of each type in every paragraph."
	Use correct spelling	"Meet with a partner to help you circle any misspelled words. Use a dictionary to fix them."

PEER FEEDBACK FORM

Name: _____ Date: _____

Questions I Have:	❏ _____ ❏ _____ ❏ _____
Feedback:	

What I'm Doing with This Feedback:

_____

_____

_____

_____

_____

_____

_____

_____

_____

_____

_____

_____

_____

_____

Libraries are important

I like going to the library to look at books it's a nice quiet place. I can pick out fifteen books to take home wit me from the liberry. Other people also go to the liberry so it is a good place to be. The libarian is always so nice to me and she helps me if i dont know how to do my homework. But i also like to go to the YMCA i can go swimming there. It is nice. Libraries help people in many different ways.

OPINION WRITING: BASIC 4TH-GRADE EXEMPLAR

Libraries are important

Have you ever gone to the library to do homework? I like going to the library to look at books it's a nice quiet place.

A new library might be a good idea. That way people can have books for free. Not everyone can buy books. I only have a few books at home and I love to read books. But at the library I can get fiftin books at a time. I like to read library books plus libraries are good because homeless people can be there.

But, a new library can help people answer questions. The benefits of libraries says that librarians answer lots of questions. We should build a new library and have more librarians. You can also look up your questions on the computer.

On the other hand, a new library could help people who want to use the internet. There are computers at libraries and I love to use the computers. Sometimes I play games on the computers. Other times I look up information. But i also like to go to the YMCA i can go swimming there. It is nice.

Libraries help people in many different ways. We should build a new library.

OPINION WRITING: PROFICIENT 4TH-GRADE EXEMPLAR

Why Our Community Needs a New Library

Have you ever gone to the library to do homework? Libraries are wonderful places that can help people with many needs. I believe a library would make a difference in our community.

A new library would help more people get the information they need. According to The Benefits of Libraries, libraries are free and have a large collection of books. And internet. This means that people who don't have many books or a computer at home can use to these important things. It also means that all kids can do research or their homework. Without a new library people wouldn't have easy access to information.

In addition, a new library would help people who have questions. According to The Benefits of Libraries "librarians answer over 6.6 million questions each week." That's a lot! Without a new library, there wouldn't be as many librarians who can help answer questions. Librarians can help with questions about books, computers, and even health insurance. So, librarians are important.

Finally, a new library could help people stay healthy. There are many programs held at libraries that help people stay healthy. acording to The Benefits of Libraries, sometimes fitness classes may be held at libraries. Not everyone has money to spend on a gym. Free library classes help them stay healthy. plus, people can learn about health programs. They can use the library's computers and internet to learn about them.

Libraries provide many helpful services for our comunity. A new library would make a big difference in our community. Let's start planning our new library today!

OPINION WRITING: ADVANCED 4TH-GRADE EXEMPLAR

Why Our Community Needs a New Library

Have you ever gone to the library to do homework? Or maybe you used a library computer. Libraries are wonderful places that can help people with many needs. For this reason, I believe a library would make the most difference in our community.

A new library would help more people get the information they need. This could help our community. "The Benefits of Libraries" says libraries are free and have a large collection of books. Plus, they have internet access. This means that people who don't have many books or a computer at home can use these important things at the library. It also means that all kids can do research or their homework assignments. Without a new library, people wouldn't have easy access to information.

Another reason a new library would help our community is that they help people find jobs. According to "My Library", many people use the library internet to find jobs. Besides, librarians may help people write a resume or fill out a job application. If we want people in our community to have jobs, we should build a new library.

In addition, a new library would help people who have questions. According to "The Benefits of Libraries", "librarians answer over 6.6 million questions each week." That's a lot of questions! Without a new library, there wouldn't be as many librarians who can help answer questions. Librarians can help with questions about books, computers, and more. So, librarians are an important part of the community. A new library would mean more librarians to help everyone.

Finally, a new library could help people stay healthy. There are many programs held at libraries that help people stay healthy. According to "The Benefits of Libraries", some libraries have fitness classes. Not everyone has money to spend on the gym. So, free library classes help them stay healthy. Plus, people can learn about health programs. They can use the library's computers and internet to learn about them. If our community wants to be healthy, we should build a new library to help reach this goal.

Libraries provide many helpful services for our community. A new library would make a big difference in providing access to information. Plus, a new library would make more space for homeless people. It would also help people answer their questions, and make our community healthier. Let's start planning our new library now!

STUDENT-FRIENDLY OPINION RUBRIC

	4 – Advanced	3 – Proficient	2 – Basic	1 – Below Basic
Focus: What is your opinion?	I introduced my topic with a clear claim. I stayed focused on my claim the entire time, and I made sure my opinion was clear in each supporting paragraph.	I introduced my topic with a claim. I stayed on topic the whole time. My reader can easily figure out my opinion.	I introduced my topic with a claim, but it is unclear. My reader can figure out my opinion, but I got off topic a few times.	I did not introduce my topic or make a claim. I did not stay focused, and it is difficult for my reader to figure out my opinion.
Organization: Why should your reader agree with you?	I was very careful about the order I wrote my paragraphs. I kept related ideas together in paragraphs. The order of my paragraphs helps my reader know what is most important to me.	I made sure to organize my writing and put related ideas together into paragraphs. The order I wrote my paragraphs in helps my reader understand my opinion better.	I tried to stay organized, but some of my ideas should be in different paragraphs. I did not put my paragraphs in a particular order.	I did not make an effort to organize my writing.
Elaboration: What evidence and commentary back you up?	I have clear reasons that are supported by relevant facts and details. I did research to add evidence to ideas I already had.	I supported my reasons with facts and details. I used evidence from research to support my reasons.	I supported my reasons, but I did not use much evidence from research. Most of my support comes from my own ideas.	I did not support my reasons. I did not do any research.
Language and Vocabulary: Make your ideas clear	I used transition words and phrases in a natural way to clarify the relationship between the claim and reasons. I revised my work to use complex words that make my writing easier to understand.	I used transition words and phrases to link my opinion and reasons. I revised my work to use some complex words that make my writing easier to understand.	I used transition words and phrases, but they feel forced, or I used them incorrectly. I revised my writing, but my vocabulary is basic, and I could have done more to make it better.	I did not use any transition words or phrases. My vocabulary is vague. I did not revise my work to make it better or use more complex words.
Conventions: Make it correct	I edited my work so well that there are no errors left.	I edited my work and took care of most of my original mistakes.	I edited my work, but I left a lot of mistakes.	I did not edit my work, and there are a lot of mistakes that need to be fixed.

WRITING RUBRIC SCORING GUIDE

The Simplify Writing® rubric is divided into five categories: Focus, Organization, Elaboration, Language & Vocabulary, and Conventions. Students receive a score for each category at one of four levels of writing: Advanced, Proficient, Basic, and Below Basic. So, the maximum score for a piece of writing is 20 points, while the lowest score a student may receive is 5 points.

While using a rubric to score writing is common practice, it can be challenging to translate these rubric scores into a number for the grade book. Traditionally, a student who receives all 4s, or 20 points, on the rubric earns a grade of 100%, while a student who receives all 2s, or 10 points, on the rubric earns a grade of 50%. However, this method of grading makes it very difficult for some writers to ever receive a passing grade.

Instead, the Simplify Writing® program recommends using a more equitable method of grading. The following chart uses a shifted scale that eliminates scores below 55%, allowing students to earn credit for their effort, and maximizes a student's potential writing score. After scoring a writing piece for each category on the rubric, add the points for each category and find the total on the chart to determine the final grade.

Writing Rubric Scoring Guide			
Rubric Score	Percentage	Rubric Score	Percentage
20	100%	12	76%
19	97%	11	73%
18	94%	10	70%
17	91%	9	67%
16	88%	8	64%
15	85%	7	61%
14	82%	6	58%
13	79%	5	55%

4th-Grade Informational Writing Sample

Koalas

Koalas might seam like cute and flufey cretchers, but there is a lot you might not know about them. A lot of the koala habitat has been destrord. So they have few trees to climb.

Koalas need lots of sleep so they can have energey. They eat the Juice in leaves. When they do this they can get energey too. Koalas have good eye sight so they can find their food. They can smell their food so they can find it this way too.

Koalas have soft fur. Their fur can keep them warm in the winter time. Kolas fur can also keep them safe. Like if they bump into somthig or fall their fur can keep them from geting hurt. And now you might know a little more about koalas.

Focus: 3; Organization: 3; Elaboration: 2;
Language & Vocabulary: 3; Conventions: 2
Total: 13 = 79%

6th-Grade Argumentative Writing Sample

Yes they should. Some kids uses a lot of screen time, some not so much. But its up to parents to decide if there kids should. So they should limiting it to like 2 hours a day. They can watch a little TV and use there phone but then needs to turn it off. Or if they are doing something educatonal for school thatis okay. Need to have a limitt so they don't uses it too much.

Focus: 2; Organization: 1; Elaboration: 1;
Language & Vocabulary: 1; Conventions: 1
Total: 6 = 58%

7th-Grade Informational Writing Sample

Seattle is a popular place to visit. It's one of my favorite vacation spots. Located in northwest Washington. There are a lot of interesting and unique things to do in Seattle so, many tourists travel there every year.

One of the most popular places to visit in Seattle is Pike Place Market. There are a lot of shops where you can go shopping. They also have a fish market, they sell fresh seafood. So visitors can go shopping and eat seafood at the restaurants. They have shrimp, lobster, and all different kinds of seafood to try. I love shopping there with my mom everytime we visit. We always get shrimp for dinner when we go to the Pike Place Market.

Tourists can also visit the Space Needle in Seattle. This is a really tall building where you can look out over the whole town. There is an elevator so, you don't have to walk up the stairs if you don't want to. The Space Needle has an observation deck you will have a great view of the entire city. It is the highest building in Seattle.

In conclusion, Seattle is a great place to visit.

Focus: 3; Organization: 4; Elaboration: 2;
Language & Vocabulary: 3; Conventions: 4
Total: 16 = 88%

ABOUT THE AUTHOR

April Smith is an experienced educator and author known for her innovative teaching resources that promote 21st-century learning concepts. With over a decade of teaching experience, April began her career in 2008 and quickly developed a passion for creating engaging educational materials to share with fellow teachers.

Her teaching resources, which include project-based learning activities such as interactive notebooks, escape games, and other content-focused lessons, have been widely recognized for their ability to ignite students' excitement for learning. April's approach to education emphasizes joyful and interactive learning experiences that keep students actively engaged in the classroom.

In 2015, April was awarded Intermediate Teacher of the Year in her county, acknowledging her exceptional teaching skills and dedication to her students' success. Her expertise in writing instruction led her to become a trainer for new elementary teachers in her district in 2015, and she expanded her reach by providing online training for teachers beginning in 2017. During the Covid-19 pandemic, April worked tirelessly with over 5,000 teachers to help them transition their writing instruction online, ensuring that students did not experience learning gaps during these challenging times.

Since 2017, April has trained over 50,000 teachers on effective writing instruction, both in-person and online, making a significant impact on education communities nationwide. Her passion for teaching and her commitment to empowering fellow educators have earned her a reputation as a leader in the field of education. April Smith continues to inspire teachers and students alike with her innovative approaches to teaching and learning.

ACKNOWLEDGMENTS

I've learned that nothing meaningful can be done without the support of others. I can't say thank you enough to everyone who has been a part of my journey as an educator and as an author.

A huge thank-you goes to Myranda McDonald, Laura Jones, and Rebecca Riddle for helping me refine the systems and create simple organizers for teachers to use in their classrooms. Thank you for helping in whatever way you could during this process, even if it was just talking through something. I'd like to also extend my gratitude to two of my youngest helpers, Kate and Sam Jones, who helped recreate the student samples for this book. Thank you to Sheri Coffman for ensuring that the teachers we work with still got the support they needed while I was focusing on writing this book. To Christy Smith, thank you for turning my boring charts into engaging illustrations.

To our 10,000 (and growing) teachers inside the Simplify Writing® program, this book wouldn't exist without you. Five years ago, I ran a beta-test with just 300 teachers to formally try out the writing curriculum I had been creating for the past six years. Their feedback was instrumental in refining the curriculum and making it a game-changer for students and teachers across the country. Many of you have advocated for a bigger focus on writing instruction at your schools, and I am so proud of you for this.

To Norine Bowers, who saw what I was trying to do by making writing a focus in my classroom and encouraged me to share it with other teachers schoolwide and at the district level. Your supportiveness made a world of difference for my students. You understood that no one teacher has the same needs, and you supported us all in different ways. I'm truly grateful to you for helping me see my potential as both a teacher and a leader.

I also want to recognize Carrie Jones, a local first-grade teacher. Thank you for taking the time to "geek out" about literacy instruction with me. I appreciate you inviting me into your classroom and sharing your passion with me. You gave me valuable insight into what teaching the foundations looks like for beginning writers. Most of all, thank you for your tireless work with my own budding writers.

And finally, a heartfelt thanks goes out to the people who really made this happen, my family. Juggling writing a book and running a business while being a mom is not for the faint of heart. I couldn't have done it without my husband being there to handle all the things I didn't have the bandwidth for. My twins had a great time going to the trampoline park, zoo, and any other activities my husband could think of to give me more time to write over the weekend. Although they enjoyed those activities, they still missed having Mom there to enjoy it with them. Thank you, Peter, Oliver, and Kira, for always understanding and supporting the projects that are important to me.

When I first pitched this book, I made it clear that my No. 1 priority was to provide as many examples and lessons as possible for teachers to easily put these systems in place. This was way more than we could print in this book, so I created a members-only area on my website for teachers to access all the materials linked in this book. Creating an account is free, and there's no book code needed.

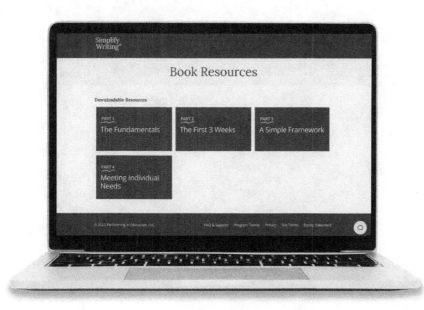

The link icon (🔗) means there is a downloadable resource available that goes with the chapter. You can create a free account and access these resources by visiting: https://www.simplifywriting.com/book-resources.

WORKS CITED

Boswell, Kelly. 2020. *Every Kid a Writer: Strategies That Get Everyone Writing*. Portsmouth, NH: Heinemann.

Brookhart, Susan M. 2017. *How to Give Effective Feedback to Your Students*. 2nd ed. Alexandria, Virginia: Ascd.

Burden, Paul. 2020. *Classroom Management: Creating a Successful K–12 Learning Community*. Hoboken, NJ: Wiley.

Farah, Kareem. 2021. "How to Set Up Mastery-Based Grading in Your Classroom." *Cult of Pedagogy*. March 7, 2021. https://www.cultofpedagogy.com/mastery-based-grading/.

Feldman, Joe. 2018. *Grading for Equity*. Corwin Press.

Fenner, Diane, and Sydney Snyder. 2017. *Unlocking English Learners' Potential*. Corwin Press.

Graham, Steve. 2019. "Changing How Writing Is Taught." *Review of Research in Education* 43 (1): 277–303. https://doi.org/10.3102/0091732x18821125.

Hammond, Zaretta. 2015. *Culturally Responsive Teaching and the Brain: Promoting Authentic Engagement and Rigor among Culturally and Linguistically Diverse Students*. Thousand Oaks, CA: Corwin.

National Center for Education Statistics. 2021. "COE – Students with Disabilities." Nces.ed.gov. May 2021. https://nces.ed.gov/programs/coe/indicator/cgg.

Schunk, Dale H., and Carl W. Swartz. 1993. *Goals and Progress Feedback: Effects on Self-Efficacy and Writing Achievement*. ERIC. https://eric.ed.gov/?id=ED359216.

Serravallo, Jennifer. 2021. *Teaching Writing in Small Groups*. Portsmouth, NH: Heinemann.

Snyder, Sydney, and Diane Staehr Fenner. 2021. *Culturally Responsive Teaching for Multilingual Learners: Tools for Equity*. Thousand Oaks, California: Corwin.

Tomlinson, Carol A. 2017. *How to Differentiate Instruction in Academically Diverse Classrooms*. 3rd ed. Moorabbin, Victoria: Hawker Brownlow Education.

Tomlinson, Carol Ann, and Jay McTighe. 2006. *Integrating Differentiated Instruction & Understanding by Design: Connecting Content and Kids*. Alexandria, VA: Ascd.

Venables, Daniel R. 2014. *How Teachers Can Turn Data into Action*. Alexandria, VA: Ascd.

Weaver, Constance. 1996. *Teaching Grammar in Context*. Portsmouth, NH: Boynton/Cook Publishers.

Zerwin, Sarah M. 2020. *Point-Less: An English Teacher's Guide to More Meaningful Grading*. Portsmouth, NH: Heinemann.

INDEX

Page numbers followed by *t* refer to tables.

Several years ago, I used the researched-based systems in this book to create the writing curriculum I always wanted as an elementary classroom teacher. This curriculum has grown using feedback from the over 10,000 teachers and 200-plus schools who have implemented it. If you are interested in putting these systems into place without having to plan any lessons yourself, I encourage you to learn more about our curriculum by visiting simplifywriting.com. You can join as an individual teacher, or we can help you get access with school funds.

Simplify Writing® is the only curriculum that provides engaging resources and differentiation materials that help teachers fill in learning gaps and empower their students to share their opinions and ideas. We include a full library to help support English Language Learners, tools for students with learning disabilities, and training on every part of the system in this book using our resources. You also get access to each day's mini-lesson for every unit, grammar and intervention lessons for small groups, and support materials for your students like audio read-alouds of our models and reading passages.

While you're checking out our curriculum on simplifywriting.com, you can also enroll in my free 90-minute workshop on engagement strategies. This training is called "How to Engage Every Student in Writing." This workshop pairs well with both this book and our curriculum. There's also a special bonus unit at the end for everyone who attends.

It would be an honor to continue to support you and your students with the Simplify Writing® program!